A NEW JEWISH THEOLOGY IN THE MAKING

BOOKS BY EUGENE B. BOROWITZ
Published by The Westminster Press

A New Jewish Theology
in the Making

A Layman's Introduction
to Religious Existentialism

A NEW JEWISH THEOLOGY IN THE MAKING

by

EUGENE B. BOROWITZ

THE WESTMINSTER PRESS
Philadelphia

LIBRARY OF CONGRESS CATALOG CARD NO. 68-25395

BOOK DESIGN BY
DOROTHY ALDEN SMITH

Published by The Westminster Press ®
Philadelphia, Pennsylvania

PRINTED IN THE UNITED STATES OF AMERICA

To My Parents

BENJAMIN AND MOLLY BOROWITZ

PREFACE

Most people seem to believe that theologies come to be in a sudden insight which is as overwhelming as it is definitive. That may be the experience of mystics but it is not common to theologians. Ideas seem to need time to grow, and the thinker himself must slowly find a way to outgrow what he was taught but knows no longer will do. Today the problem of finding a fresh way in theology has become almost paralyzingly difficult. Every competent thinker knows the many options that have been tried in several faiths in our time and the intense criticism each has received. Every mental move he makes, therefore, is attended by the most intense self-consciousness. Not this or that doctrine prompts fundamental questions but the very method of doing the work. Where to begin, how to proceed, what shape the whole shall be given, are all critical problems, for each decision affects the very substance of the faith involved.

These observations apply with special force to that minority concern in a minority faith, creating a theology of Judaism. The first effort in such a project must be to confront the previous works in this area. By assessing what remains valid in them and where they need to be surpassed, one may hope to find one's own approach to meeting the methodological challenge. This volume presents a survey of my efforts at such reflection. Because method, much less substance, is not gained without trial and reconsideration, my procedural hypotheses have been tested over the years by being applied to a variety of topics with which a Jewish theology should be concerned. Hence the approach arrived at in this book, though it can stand on its own internal, intellectual foundations as presented here, will be more fully understood in terms of the substantive studies which were being carried on at the same time. These studies form my companion volume, *How Can a Jew Speak of Faith Today?* which will appear shortly.

My overriding concern in these investigations has been to respond to the contemporary religious experience of the people of Israel as best I can understand it. That, if such a thing may be said, is the Biblical way of working at the theological task. Of course, only a prophet could hope to know with some certainty who indeed are the faithful remnant amid the confusions we call history. I have no such special vision. I only know I must take my stand where I find myself and where I find a not insignificant fraction of my people gathering. We are that group who, having stampeded from Jewish tradition into general culture, now find it a higher wisdom to reclaim our stake in our traditional faith. Having gone as far into contemporary intellectuality as we have, we now realize we cannot base our Jewish theology on science, philosophy, or the mood of the times even as we still cannot found it on verbal revelation. Contemporary Christianity may be agog over securality. Since we were in it up to the nostrils for several decades, we know we are men of faith precisely because we must move beyond it. We obviously do not believe as much as our grandfathers did, but we have discovered painfully that we believe far more than our society does. We are searching for a way to explain the truth we are trying to live, even though it is difficult to believe such a thing can be given intellectual structure today. Nonetheless—that great Jewish theological term—the effort must be made.

A further word is in order concerning the mode of address employed here. It is based on a conscious dissent from the requirement of academic prose that the writer encourage the reader to remain detached and distant from the material. If the existentialists have taught us anything, it is that faith is a matter of the whole self. In that case, writing which carefully restricts itself so as to appeal only to the mind cannot hope to communicate the depth of religious belief. That thesis must not be permitted to become a rationalization for sloppy intellectuality in description, criticism, or proposal. A mindless self is a contradiction in terms. Yet the rigid academic stance is often insisted upon in religious matters to guarantee that faith will make no claims upon one where one really lives. I therefore try to write about theological matters in an informed and thoughtful way, yet with a greater concern to arouse the whole man to what I believe is at stake.

I wish here to record my deep indebtedness to Mrs. Robert Paxton for her intelligent and diligent secretarial assistance; to the staff of The Westminster Press for unfailing courtesy and thoughtful guidance; and to my wife, Estelle, for the special efforts which made possible this book, as so much else. I conclude with the words of the traditional morning blessing:

בָּרוּךְ אַתָּה יְיָ אֱלֹהֵינוּ מֶלֶךְ הָעוֹלָם הַנּוֹתֵן לַיָּעֵף כֹּחַ

Adonai our God, King of the Universe, I call you blessed for giving strength to the weary.

EUGENE B. BOROWITZ

Hebrew Union College
Jewish Institute of Religion
The New York School

ACKNOWLEDGMENTS

GRATEFUL ACKNOWLEDGMENT is herewith made for permission to use the following material:

"Jewish Faith and the Jewish Future," from *Great Jewish Ideas*, ed. by Abraham E. Millgram, B'nai B'rith Book Series, Vol. V, published by B'nai B'rith's Commission on Adult Jewish Education, 1640 Rhode Island Ave., N.W., Washington, D.C.

"Crisis Theology and the Jewish Community" and "The Jewish Need for Theology," from *Commentary*, July, 1961, and August, 1962. Copyright © 1961 and © 1962 respectively by the American Jewish Committee.

"The Legacy of Martin Buber," from *Union Seminary Quarterly Review*, Broadway at 120th St., New York, N.Y., Vol. XXII, No. 1 (November, 1966).

"The Typological Theology of Joseph Baer Soloveitchik," from *Judaism*, Spring, 1966.

"Faith and Method in Modern Jewish Theology," and "Autonomy Versus Tradition," Central Conference of American Rabbis *Yearbook*, 1963, and *Journal*, April, 1968.

CONTENTS

Part Three

IN SEARCH OF A STANCE

EPILOGUE

Part One

HIS PEOPLE, STILL AND DESPITE

1

SURVIVAL AND SELF-UNDERSTANDING

ANYONE who has lived through the past thirty years has seen the great constructive change that has swept over American Jewry. Together with its brother Jews in many but, sadly, not in all corners of the world, American Jewry, both leading and led, as patron and as beneficiary, has attained such Jewish self-respect that it seeks positive and creative ways of living its Jewishness. Much of its concern today is: What does it mean to live a modern Jewish life? How can we do so?

Nothing could be more astonishing or more significant after what Jews have suffered. The disaster of European Jewry had no precedent in the long history of Jewish pain, nor in the perversities of modern civilization. That one out of every three living Jews was killed for no other reason than that he was a Jew, even when he had only the most peripheral connection with Jewry, should have been enough to make the rest of Jewry resign from history. And the exterminated Jewish communities were the human source and the spiritual standard of all the other Jewish settlements in the world. What organism can survive such a loss of heart and head?

Had this destruction been the work of invading barbarians, the chance effect of an uncontrollable epidemic or natural catastrophe, the Jews might simply have endured and, the visitation past, returned to normal existence. But can there ever again be "normal" existence for Jews? The Germans were not a nation of primitive and illiterate men but among the most educated and civilized of the twentieth century. They did not kill Jews in sporadic outbursts of uncontainable rage or unaccountable accident. They killed coldly, out of mature reflection, with deliberate intent, by industrial methods and in hope of leaving no survivors. That the Germans could do such a thing was literally incredible—that they did so is an irreducible fact of future Jewish history. Moreover, the extent to which the democratic nations might have helped but did not or would not still burns and sears and brands the Jewish psyche.

The attitude of the non-Jewish world cannot be taken lightly. The existence of modern Jewry is dependent upon its good will. That is an obvious fact for Jewish communities, such as the American, which participate intimately in the lives of the nations. The survival of the State of Israel is equally dependent on the active help or passive acquiescence of the great powers.

Are the nations today trustworthy? World Jewry, with its people ravaged and its confidence in educated, democratic man shattered beyond reconstruction, had every right after World War II to refuse to go on. By willful and conscious personal assimilation, by ceasing to do anything more about being Jewish, by the easiest sort of drift into the large anonymous masses of modern society, out of disgust, rebellion, exhaustion, or weariness, the Jews, in a generation or two, could have quit. Hitler, though defeated, would have won. Perhaps that in itself is the major though unconscious reason why the Jews, once again, refused to be reasonable. The revival of world Jewry is the Jewish, morally spiteful insistence that Hitler's defeat must be complete.

After the war, the overwhelming majority of Jews refused to capitulate. The European survivors were an awe-inspiring example of that will-to-live as Jews. Shortly after the concentration camps were liberated, weddings were celebrated, economic enterprises begun, organizations founded, and protests and debate, those steady signs of Jewish vitality, abounded.

This was more than an animal instinct for survival. It stemmed from that deep-felt belief, fostered and ingrained by Jewish observance, that life comes from God and is good, that living is the indispensable means to holiness, and that holiness is reached in life, not beyond it.

The years following the war required Jews to build a new Jewishness, to bring into being a more significant and fulfilling Jewish life than had hitherto existed. It was not the Jewish love of life alone that erupted but that fundamental Jewish sense of responsibility, that messianic thrust, that impelled and powered them as well.

Two great accomplishments resulted which epitomize the miraculous result. A Jewish state was reestablished in the Land of Israel. Years of familiarity have dulled the memory of nearly two thousand years of waiting and weeping, and fifty years of intense political and cultural effort. The great nations may have allowed the State to come into being, but it was Jewish sweat, talent, and blood that created and sustained it. No communal Jewish effort since Biblical days can be compared to it.

Less spectacular but equally providential has been the extraordinary maturation of the American Jewish community. Adversity in Europe meant responsibility here. American Jewry accepted its duties and grew to new stature in fulfilling them. The record of rescue and rehabilitation, of political agitation and support, is in the noblest traditions of Jewish brotherliness. Many doubt that an instance of equally generous communal *tzedakah*, "charity," can be found in the annals of Jewish history.

These concerns for the welfare of other Jews brought a new and searching concern for the future of American Jewry itself. Working and giving for other Jews meant acknowledging one's Jewish identity and a commitment to act upon it. Increasingly, that consciousness turned inward and asked what it meant to be a Jew in the United States, what should be done to make

American Jewish life more meaningful and significant. That most American Jews today live in a quiet pride of Jewishness, that American Jewishness is stronger, richer, more varied in program and higher in standards than anyone would have dared estimate before World War II, are measures of the startling suddenness with which what seemed barely in bud has now come into flower.

This recitation of achievement is not meant to deny the serious problems which still exist in Jewish life. To discuss Jewish hope is not to be blind to the perils of Jewish life but rather to focus on those aspects which the Jew views with some confidence.

The postwar resurgence of Jewry was not a response to a great, dramatic personality who in his person, by his deeds or speeches, summoned forth all the energies left in this tried and tired people. Nor was it channeled through an intellectual movement which by its analysis so explained what had happened and so justified what yet was to be that this people, despite its physical debilitation, felt constrained to move forward. Nor was it the result of any organization whose program was so appealing that the Jews seized it as the fulfillment of their Jewish needs. This is not to underestimate the importance of either the rescue or Zionist organizations. Both did an invaluable job in Europe, but they did not so much lead the people as respond to their needs; they did not create the desire for life and the will to emigrate, but nobly took advantage of an opportunity. Their greatness is that they were ready and responsive to a people which had itself already made the basic decision.

The hero of the postwar period is *the Jewish people itself*. Without prophet or lawgiver, without a great book or dominant school of philosophy, without benefit of worldwide resolutions, conventions, declarations, or press releases, it determined to survive Jewishly and in honor. That basic will-to-be-Jewish has characterized the Jews in the past two decades and has been responsible for the remarkable change in the content and tone of Jewish life. Because its roots are deeper than a man, a concept, or an organization, because it is a widespread and pervasive phenomenon, it must be understood in proper depth. The believing Jew will approach this phenomenon with a certain awe, recognizing here another of those exodus experiences which characterize the uncanny history of this holy people, or, in brief, the saving hand of God.

For the moment at least, the Jewish people is conscious of and interested in its Jewishness. Discussions of the Jewish future are not hypothetical but concrete, not *whether* it will be but what it will be.

How Jewish life has changed in the United States in the past twenty-five or thirty years! Self-hatred, or at least ambivalence, dominated in the thirties, the decade of the furtive changing of names, the straightening of noses, the suppression of accents and gestures, the cultivation of non-Jewish manners and non-Jewish approval. Though some of these symptoms are still to be found, negative attributes no longer characterize today's Jews. They are, on the whole, self-accepting. They know that they are Jewish, and assume that others know and respect them for it. And they do not hesitate to do some things, at least, that identify them with the Jewish community. Their children, too, are growing up with the notion that it is natural to be a Jew. They have not had the traumas most of their parents experienced in discovering their Jewish identity. (As the next decade or two brings these children to maturity their advent may itself be anticipated with hope.)

The immediate temptation in analyzing American Jewish life is to deal with its organizations and their programs. But a catalog of them would be dull and unrealistic. The great American Jewish organizations do not lead Jewish life but, rather, try to keep up with what the community seems to want. That is why their activities overlap and compete. Hence, an analysis of the positive patterns of Jewish existence in America is better done in social and intellectual terms, a description of what Jews in real Jewish communities in different parts of the United States are doing. To make the various possibilities clear, three major levels of activity have artificially been isolated—social, cultural, and religious.

The most peripheral form of Jewish association is probably that which exists for the sake of self-defense. At one time this was a major preoccupation of American Jewry. In the 1930's anti-Semitism was open, active, and supported by non-Jews of stature and influence. Though positive Jewishness meant little to many, the fear of those who hated Jews made many a Jew cooperate with his coreligionists in self-protection. The post-war era has seen a radical decline in the extent, intensity, and influence of anti-Semitism. What exists openly is a disreputable and lunatic fringe. Such pressure as the Jew feels today is largely social in character in terms of clubs, neighborhoods, and cliques, though there is always the threat of something more serious.

Despite these changes, some Jews make their appearance only when the subject of defense is involved. Their caricature is the well-known figure who is active in interfaith activities but has no real faith of his own. There are those, however, who convert the acceptance of their destiny into a moral virtue. For them the fight for Jewish rights is a means of realizing democracy. Leaving the Jewish people while it is embattled is cowardice, working with it the least a decent man can do. Such ethical self-respect is admirable but it cannot build a Jewish way of life.

More positive is the uncomplicated assertion of those Jews who like Jews and who prefer to associate with them. No deep philosophic necessity drives them to buy a home near other Jews, to join a Jewish club, to send their children to a non-sectarian but obviously Jewish camp, or to make their reservations at resorts frequented by other Jews. They feel more comfortable with Jews; they enjoy being with "their own kind."

No one has ever tried to estimate how widespread this sense of Jewish sociability is, nor are there any standards by which to measure its strength. Nonetheless, the American Jewish community today would be unrecognizable without its operation. Its expression ranges through the use of Yiddish or other "inside" Jewish expressions, the enjoyment of Jewish jokes, the preference for Jewish foods, the joining of Jewish social or recreational clubs, the insistence, for reasons otherwise unclear, upon marriage within the community, up to the vague assertion that one simply prefers the Jewish style of living.

When conviviality is the honest choice of those who genuinely prefer people of similar backgrounds, standards, and interests, it is difficult to deny its legitimacy. When, as still happens, Jews huddle together from an archaic, tribal fear of the outsider, the *goy*, that is a counterprejudice, but a prejudice nonetheless and therefore deserving elimination, not preservation. Still, Jewish fraternity can hardly serve as a central motive for the life of American Jewry. It arose as the by-product of a deeper unity which held the generations together in their pursuit of a great historic goal. What will create that feeling as the generations pass if there is nothing else to give rise to it but the memory of previous generations' conviviality? As democracy becomes practice and Jews are socially more welcome among their non-Jewish neighbors, what will sustain the Jewish community? Is good fellowship all that remains of the noble Jewish tradition?

Many Jews have responded to these questions by hitching their social needs to some worthy Jewish purpose in the form of a Jewish organization. This is not entirely an American phenomenon, though the American mania for organizations and conventions is well known. Jews of the Middle Ages also had societies, the *hevrah*, whose function might be burying the dead, marrying off eligible but indigent Jewish maidens, the study of the Talmud, visiting the sick. Nor did they get together only to fulfill their stated goal. Their records are full of meetings, feasts, and celebrations. Thus the host of organizations which may be found in even the smallest American Jewish community today has distinguished forebears. When the Jewish will-to-be-sociable is linked to "a good cause," the American Jew finds it difficult to resist.

Most Jewish organizations may speedily be recognized for what they are: "moral fronts" for Jewish enjoyment. The American Jewess apparently does not feel quite right about spending afternoons at fashion shows or card parties, and her husband has a similar anxiety about spending evenings bowling, watching a magician, or listening to a sports celebrity. Let these activities be connected with a worthy Jewish cause and the guilt is expiated.

Projects of mutual Jewish concern and value are pursued with devotion and accomplishment by many organizations. The most consistently praiseworthy are the local combined charity appeals, the international rescue and State of Israel aid programs. Here, at least, the interminable dinners, the ego-serving awards, and the social pressure to give serve significant Jewish ends. They not only keep the American Jewish community organized and alive, they mean life or death to Jews in many another land.

In the less dramatic but equally significant work of the Jewish communal agencies at home, settlement houses and vocational agencies have more and more been replaced with personal and family counseling or services to the aging. These are but the most evident of the professionally staffed, morally oriented programs of high standard which American Jews have created and carried on for their brothers.

At this level there is surely positive reason for Jewish life and action. Jews need and want to help one another. Through a voluntary system unmatched in human history they have done so and will continue to do so. For many Jews such praiseworthy concerns with organized mutual help are sufficient reason for their active participation in and loyalty to the Jewish people.

Tzedakah, "charity," has been lauded by Jewish sages through the centuries, and the American Jew has learned to practice it on a grand, international scale. No realistic Jew can cavil at its importance but questions can and must be asked about *tzedakah* as the sole or central concern of American Jewish existence. Whence does the extraordinary concern of Jew for brother Jew arise? Whence the motive to give generously for distant and unknown souls? *Tzedakah* may have special appeal to Jews but, like Jewish fellowship, it is but one product of a deeper sense of duty and obligation. With governments increasingly entering the welfare field, with Jews integrating more intimately into American society, the worthy practice of Jewish charity cannot alone power American Jewry but is itself in need of strengthening.

A more positive foundation and indeed an understanding of all Jewish activity is offered to the American Jew by the cultural and religious interpretations of Jewish living.

The term "Jewish culture" once encompassed a lively array of divergent approaches to Jewish life. Today the living options are limited to two, the educational and the Zionist.

In the 1920's, when the great masses of large-city Jewry were still fresh from Central and Eastern Europe, and still in the thirties when accommodation to American culture was slowly making headway, a variety of Jewish cultural theses were propounded and lived. Jewish socialism claimed the allegiance of thousands whom it enlisted in the cause of human betterment through political action. Carried out in the Yiddish language and appealing to the historic memories and prophetic concerns of the Jewish people, it seemed an extraordinarily worthy fusion of the Jewish past with the needs of contemporary man. Even its opposition to Zionism and religion could not dim its appeal, though little of the movement remains today (except for the Yiddish daily newspaper *Der Forverts*). Closely allied to and often indistinguishable from it was the Jewish labor movement. Here the old Jewish concern for justice and opportunity took the form of organizing unions among the Jewish working class. Since substantial numbers of immigrants were laborers, concentrated largely in the needle trades, it seemed as if a major portion of metropolitan Jewry could be involved in the struggle for social justice. Though these unions today may retain their Jewish leadership, their Jewish members are retiring in increasing numbers and have for some years been outnumbered by rural Southern, Italian, Negro, and Puerto Rican recruits.

Applying a full-scale philosophy of Judaism in its program, the secular Yiddishist or Yiddish nationalist movement took a number of organizational forms, the chief survivor of which is the Sholom Aleichem Folk School movement. The ideology of the various groups was roughly similar: though Jewish existence could not be based on religion because of the growth of modern science, the Jewish heritage still had much to say to modern man in his search for a rich existence.

According to these secularists, the fundamental problem of modern Jewishness lay in its misinterpretation of the nature of the Jewish group. While religion had been its major concern in the Middle Ages, that had been only one part of a folk existence. The Jews survived not because of their faith but because the governments under which they had lived had always granted them a measure of autonomy. They had collected their own taxes, operated their own courts and provided their own educational system. In Eastern Europe, where this theory originated, many nationality groups lived within one state and continued their own ethnic cultures. The Yiddishists felt that though the United States Government did not officially recognize such folk communities, the Jews should voluntarily create and operate their separate folk life, thus enriching the total American culture.

In opposition to the Zionists, the Yiddishists turned their backs on the Land of Israel and its language. They argued that mankind was moving toward greater unity, beyond the sovereignty of individual states and toward internationalism. The

Jews were really the first cosmopolitan nation, an example of the way in which national groups should reach a transgeographic, moral, and humanistic level. Yiddish being the living, functioning language of this people, it should be fostered and extended through research, creativity, and usage. The hope was that through the creation of a Yiddish-centered culture, the American Jew would be both simultaneously a man of the modern world and a significant inheritor and progenitor of the Jewish tradition.

The breadth and daring of this effort to reconstruct contemporary Judaism must still inspire respect, though social developments have rendered it almost completely impractical. With most American Jews now native-born, the use of Yiddish has largely disappeared. The serious Yiddish theater is down to a weekend, museum showcase in New York, and literary creativity of quality is better found in South America where more recent immigration and Latin exclusiveness have kept Yiddish alive. Today's advertisements for the Sholom Aleichem Folk Schools in the suburbs offer a secular Jewish education to those who cannot find themselves at home in the synagogue, but also provide for a "secular Bar Mitzvah" (*sic!*).

Much of what remains of the once strong Jewish secularist movements now finds its outlets in that ill-defined cluster of attitudes which center about the desire "to give my child a Jewish education." This is perhaps the clearest, most self-conscious, most intense and direct Jewish concern of the American Jew.

Why the American Jew should feel so strongly about this matter is not clear even to himself. On the whole he is dissatisfied with his own Jewish education, but that paradoxically has led him to want his child to have a better one. Even if he is not religiously observant or Hebraically informed, he still wants his child to know that tradition and its language. Many parents also feel that should their children ever face anti-Semitism they should know why they are Jews.

Aside from either the Zionist or religious justifications of education, some parents and many educators take a cultural approach to Jewish schooling. At its simplest level they can speak of Jewish ethics, the importance of teaching the child that positive, activist, demanding attitude to human relations which is peculiarly the fruit of Jewish thought and experience and has been embodied in Jewish practice. Some speak of Jewish values, whose larger perspective includes such virtues as the love of life, the appreciation of pleasure, the emphasis on rationality, the encouragement of individual worth. Others speak of the Jewish way of life, embracing not only intellectual content and folk forms, but the very people and its creativity as well. Another group wishes to transmit the Jewish heritage, that great accumulation of experience and wisdom, of books and customs, of heroes and endurance.

How positive a force this is in contemporary Jewry may be seen in the variety and growth of Jewish educational institutions, or in the pervasive dissatisfaction with what was done in the past. Since World War II the most rapidly developing sector in Jewish education has been the Jewish day school, which takes in almost 10 percent of the children currently receiving a Jewish education. A similar concern with depth has been shown in both the Conservative and Reform congregational programs. The former have not only insisted with great success on a minimum three-day-a-week program but are now engaged in an effort to extend the Bar Mitzvah training to include an early start and a high school continuation for Jewish education. The Reform Jews, who have long had better continuity in their programs, are now engaged in expanding their voluntary midweek programs, in raising the age level of confirmation and increasing the number of postconfirmation classes. Both groups have placed heavy emphasis upon summer camping and sponsor group visits to the State of Israel.

What may be the single most revealing sign of the state of Jewish education is the virtual disappearance of the "Bar

Mitzvah mill." No longer will any self-respecting congregation agree to a ceremony after three months of training. Two-year requirements are becoming minimal, with many congregations insisting upon three or four years of prior study. Since there is no authority in the Jewish community to enforce such a rule, its general observance must be attributed to its endorsement by the general will of American Jewish parenthood. This is a constructive sign, which indicates how a devotion to Jewish education, for whatever reason, strengthens and supports Jewish life in America.

The desire to educate is beyond Jewish criticism except when it is presented as a full answer to the problems of Jewish existence. Such views maintain that Jewish education is an end in itself; it requires no justification, no philosophical validation. But even if the question, Why educate? is momentarily set aside, then the question, Educate for what? immediately springs forward. No school system has enough time or its personnel enough wisdom or energy to do everything. Those who arrange its program must make decisions as to what they will and will not teach, arouse, exemplify. In these judgments a standard of Jewish values is at work. Consciously or unconsciously a philosophy of Judaism is founding and directing this plan of Jewish education. The will to educate cannot itself provide a criterion of judgment; all it can say is that the more education the better—a futile and unrealistic position, considering the realities of Jewish life and its continuing transition.

Jewish education is an absolutely indispensable means for the development of Jewish life. It is a major incentive for such devotion as the American Jewish community has already mustered. It must be continued in effort, enlarged in scope, deepened in mastery, intensified in effect and made the responsibility of every Jew, not just of his school or synagogue. But it can do so only when it serves a broad philosophy of Jewish life, not when it tries to become one itself.

Two major interpretations of Jewishness, two general theories of Judaism, remain active among thoughtful American Jews: the so-called "Zionist" and "religious" concepts. The term "Zionism" is still so deeply associated with the efforts to establish the State of Israel that to use it to describe a mode of Jewish living years later seems anachronistic. Because the word "religion" suffers from its close connection with Christian, particularly Protestant, understanding of the relationship between God and man, connoting church rather than folk, creed rather than commandment, the personal rather than the communal, it hardly seems appropriate to describe the traditional relation between God and the Jewish people. Still, the terms must be used.

Other than a frontal anti-Semitic assault, nothing so actively unifies the American Jewish community as a common interest in and concern for the State of Israel. The older generation remembers the bitter refugee years and the struggle to bring the State into being. For them the State of Israel still means the excitement of its declaration, the day its flag was hoisted at the United Nations, the arrival of the first Israeli ships in American ports, the pictures of refugees debarking at Haifa, the victory against Arab attacks. Though American Jewish youth lack this personal historic depth, they easily identify with the pioneering, embattled, humanitarian aspects of a living reality which has accompanied much of their existence. The community as a whole is still generous to causes in the State of Israel whether these be charitable or investments. This positive concern extends to the realm of education as well. American Jews want their children to know about the State. There is hardly a community of size where individuals have not already visited or are about to tour the State of Israel.

On the everyday level, to the average American Jew, "Zionism" is the web of feeling and response noted above. Some Zionist philosophers, however, continue to urge that Zionism could constitute a full pattern of Jewishness for Jews outside Israel. For implicit in the effort to create the State was a positive and creative attitude concerning the Jewish people and its life.

According to Zionism, the Jews are not primarily a religious group, though there may be many today who wish to live a Jewish religious life. For many centuries in the Middle Ages, Judaism was limited entirely to religious activities. This contraction of self-expression enabled the Jews to preserve their group nature in a difficult and trying time. But the Jews were always a folk, a people, or, in the special European sense of the term, a nation. (Those who find this usage painful should remember that connotations change. A precisely similar species of embarrassment is created today by the usage of the anti-Zionist Reform thinker Kaufmann Kohler, who, in a nineteenth-century European sense, used the word "race" to describe the Jewish group.)

Now that modern Jewry is free to be itself and since modern men have so many doubts about the value of religion, say the Zionists, Jews should express themselves in every normal avenue of national expression—land, language, government. This is what makes a state so desirable from the cultural as distinct from the humanitarian point of view. The State will not merely save Jews, it will save Judaism. It will do so not merely by preserving the best of the Jewish past but by creating new values, new patterns, new modes of Jewishness. And it will do so in a way that Diaspora Jews never can, for the Israeli need be true only to his Jewish self, not to some alien majority which will set his cultural standards. On its own land, speaking its own tongue, true to its own standards, the Jewish people can be truly Jewish at last.

For many European Zionist thinkers as for a substantial number of Israelis today, Zionism is the only real hope for Judaism in the contemporary world. The Jewish communities outside the Land are destined to disappear either by anti-Semitic outbreak or by assimilation to the majority culture. From this standpoint the great duty of Jews in the Diaspora is to immigrate or prepare themselves for immigration. Anything less would be unworthy of a desire to lead a full Jewish life.

Such theories of Zionism have never had much sway in America, as the low level of American immigration to the State of Israel indicates. American Zionists have rarely risen above their preoccupation with rescue and rehabilitation. On such occasions, they have spoken in terms of "cultural Zionism," the hope that Jewish life in the Diaspora can continue if it bases itself upon Israeli culture. The Hebrew language is the key to this cultural influence, permitting the Jew in other lands to read the novels, plays, poetry, of the gifted writers of his people. Through their essays, criticism, and discussion, he can share the intellectual excitement of the Jew speaking as a Jew, confronting the basic issues of modern society. Through their concentrated research into the Jewish past, qualitatively different from that of any other center by virtue of its existence on the land of the Bible and its at-homeness with the Hebrew tongue, he can gain new insight into his Jewish past. Their crafts, music, painting, and dance can adorn his life and inspire him in his own land to similar levels of creativity. He will not, for all of this, be any less a citizen of the culture of his native country, but his life will rather be enriched and uplifted by the special quality which Jewishness will add to his existence. This humanistic-spiritual bond with his brothers in the State of Israel will all the more effectively bind him to Jews in every part of the world and tie him to their common purposes. The Jewish people can live not only on its land, but through its land, elsewhere as well.

Through this concern, or something akin to it, a wide range of projects has been sponsored in the American Jewish community. Most obvious is the devotion given to the teaching of Hebrew to adults as well as to children, not just as a classic tongue but as the living language of a living people. Those trained in the old *ba, bo, be, bi* method of learning Hebrew will be surprised to find today's teachers using the full panoply of modern teaching devices from tapes and records to language laboratories and teaching machines. Some communities have experimented with teaching Hebrew via television. The Hebrew-speaking summer camp, the Hebrew high school, and the teachers' college are respected community efforts, and the summer, semester, or year spent in Israel is common.

The broader cultural exchange has touched far wider circles in the community. Visiting Israeli artists regularly appear in most reasonably large American cities, while the largest are graced by the great Israeli ensembles, the Symphony, Habimah Theatre, and the Inbal Dancers. Records of Israeli folk songs are widely produced and purchased. Israeli crafts are found in many an American Jewish home. Courses and lectures on the State, its geography, politics, peoples, and problems are frequent and well received. Israel folk dance groups, *halil* classes, folk song sessions are not uncommon. When these diverse cultural activities are tied to the political concern and the emotional involvement of the American Jew with the State of Israel, the "Zionist" influence furthering the maturation of the American Jewish community can be seen as a living force.

Some Zionists still believe that this incipient cultural renaissance will grow to the point of a full-scale foundation for Jewish life in the United States. The overwhelming majority of American Jews, however, seem to be moving in another direction. While the State of Israel, its people, and to a lesser extent its culture, will always remain precious to them, it apparently cannot serve as the center of their Jewish existence in America. Membership in male Zionist organizations has declined drastically since the founding of the State, and what is left is neither youthful nor enthusiastic. Hadassah and Pioneer Women manage better because of their "good causes." Most Hebrew courses end with few in attendance; the number reaching a second- or third-year level is small indeed. American Hebraists grow increasingly rare, and most realistic American educators admit that Hebrew will, at best, be a second tongue for only a small minority of American Jewry. Thus the readers of current Hebrew literature are few, and the creators of American Jewish plays, stories, and poems in Hebrew are largely an older, immigrant generation.

Zionist leaders both in the United States and abroad have admitted the depth of this problem by fitfully seeking to define a new statement of Zionist principles, one that would revitalize the movement and give guidance for Jewish life in the post-State era. These efforts have ended in futility, or in other versions of the old and tired programs of the past.

Despite such criticisms, love for and concern with the State of Israel have a sure place in the future of American Judaism. Anti-Zionism, despite similar "spiritual" fanaticism on the part of ultra-Orthodox and ultra-Reform groups, is as unthinkable for most American Jews as the Zionist culture theory is impractical.

In American Jewry today, it is the "religious" interpretation of Judaism which holds the decisive place. In 1925 only 40 percent of American Jewish children enrolled in Jewish schools were being educated by congregations, with most of the remainder in communal schools whose tone was largely cultural and Zionist. By 1957, over 90 percent of children receiving a Jewish education were doing so under congregational auspices.

The phenomenon of rising religious affiliation is not confined to Jews. A similar movement has affected other religious groups in American society since the end of the war. Since the contemporary American ethos not only permits but encourages religious difference, the American Jew, whose religion is acknowledged as one of the major American faiths (an extraordinary, even providential fact), accepts religion as the chief factor in his Jewish distinctiveness. As a result, in new communities, synagogues always precede Jewish recreation facilities, and then devote themselves to the stimulation of communal, familial, and private Jewish living. There is almost no modern Jewish community whose congregations are not prime movers of much of its organized activity.

But a paradox lies at the heart of this situation. A truly religious Jewry, conscious of itself as a folk dedicated to serving

God through his commandments, would have direction and guidance, purpose and passion, for its communal and personal Jewish existence. However, for all its numbers and activity, American Jews cannot be called significantly religious. Studies of synagogue affiliation and religious beliefs make abundantly clear that most Jews join congregations for everything but religious reasons. Distance, membership costs, social standing, the personality of the rabbi, the reputation of the school: these count. Attendance at services and adult study as contrasted with social events or general meetings shows how slight is the concern with God and his law. Regardless of their denominational label, most American Jews are largely nonobservant at home and in their everyday life. Ironically, it may well be that secular Judaism, which could not dominate American Judaism under its own name, now may do so under the auspices of the synagogue. Here too the pattern is not limited to Jews but has been noted in most of American religious life.

The average synagogue and the large synagogue organizations do not redeem this situation by the example of their own religiosity. Their competition for preeminence, their preoccupation with public relations, their inability to apply to their own organization what they tell their members to do in their lives perturb and offend the sensitive believer. The American Jew may belong, but he does not believe much. His religiosity is rarely serious or profound.

Thus the paradox emerges. If the American Jew were truly religious, he would create a living American Jewish community, but though he organizes his community along religious lines, his life shows little religious belief and practice. *If he were . . .* that is the crisis of the American Jewish future and the problem which American Jewish religious leadership must meet.

For some sectors of the religious community the answer is clear. The ultra-Orthodox, for example, know that they are right, that they are doing what God wants Jews to do. While their numbers may be small, they have confidence in their way of life. This security stems not only from their observant Orthodoxy but from their refusal to deviate from the full social style of their European forebears. Dressed in the *kaftan,* adorned with *peyot,* devoted to their *rebbe,* they continue steadfastly on what they know to be the one authentic Jewish path.

All other varieties of religious Jewry feel something must be done to transform European Jewish piety into a compelling American style that is yet truly Jewish. Some limit their efforts to what has been done before, perhaps trying to do it a little better. Others seize on the technical approach, utilizing better group know-how to attract larger crowds, more participation, greater follow-up. Still others wait for some new development in general culture to justify their work. Last year it was Judaism and psychiatry, this year race relations, next year outer space. Equating performing commandments with keeping busy, they have neither time nor reason to wonder whom they are serving. There are countless creative reasons for avoiding God and his will.

To speak seriously of the religious content of Judaism is to speak of the thoughtful few. There are such thoughtful men in every wing of American Jewry. No one point of view dominates the scene or gives promise of sweeping across American Jewry. Each demands too much for many men to be speedily yet deeply converted to its truth.

On first thought the modern American-style Orthodox would seem to have the easiest task. What they propose is concrete action, not foggy spirituality; authentically Jewish, not traditionally unrecognizable; conformable to America, not alien or ghetto. If one clarifies the distinction between Jewish law and the folk patterns of Poland or Hungary, the essentials of Jewish living can be distinguished from what one or another locale has added to them. The appropriate use of English, short men's jackets, reasonable decorum in the service, are not incompatible with a life based on halachah. True Jewish life will still make special demands on the observant American Jew, but any religion which does not do so is unworthy of serious respect. The Jew who wants to be faithful to Judaism will want to observe the law that God gave on Sinai and that he has graciously allowed his sages to clarify for every succeeding generation.

The Orthodox call to the Jewish community to return to their ancestral standards in a way legitimately accommodated to this country has met with far more response in the postwar years than most non-Orthodox thinkers anticipated. The young, fully observant Jew is no longer a stranger to American Judaism and, though many have thought religion and science incompatible, the devoutly Orthodox Jewish scientist is in plentiful evidence. The growth of human knowledge has not made the tradition meaningless for such Jewish products of contemporary education and culture. Rather, knowing the best that man has to offer, they believe that God has given man the critical guidance he needs to meet the demands of modern existence, that through God's Torah modern man can live in full faith, confidence, and hope just as ancient man did.

But for all its directness and unequivocation, modern Orthodoxy faces a fundamental problem. The American Jew has abandoned traditional observance. Even when he calls himself Orthodox, his observance of the Sabbath and *kashrut,* the dietary laws, not to mention lesser laws, is generally characterized by transgression.

This lack of observance stems from the belief, inarticulated but unquestionably real, that "God doesn't really care about these details." If the modern Jew could truly believe that God himself was outraged if he flipped an electric switch on the Sabbath, ate chicken not killed by a ritual slaughterer or had less repetitive services, perhaps he would accept the holy discipline with all its benefits. But, on the whole, he remains skeptically American. He cannot imagine that God is not pleased with him when he actively seeks to be a decent human being while retaining as much of Jewish practice as he can. Orthodoxy cannot settle for such a laissez-faire attitude, but how it can bring the American Jew to revere traditional law and its observance is unclear.

The various non-Orthodox views all grant the religious validity of the American Jew's turn from fully traditional conduct. They concede that modern society requires a new statement of Jewish life, one which begins from the tradition but moves forward. What makes them liberals, in all their diversity of theory and label, is their willingness to depart from the established norms of Orthodoxy to meet the needs of a changing situation.

All of them suffer under a blanket criticism from the Orthodox, who believe there is but one Torah tradition, one genuinely Jewish way of living. To say this is not binding is, in the Orthodox view, to create a mongrel Judaism, inauthentic and untrue.

The progressive groups have sought to counter this criticism by insisting that Judaism has always changed and that their various means of change represent the best of the tradition facing the best of the new world. Most American Jews have found these arguments convincing or have been willing to accept them as rationalizations for their new way of living.

The changes introduced have made American Jews more comfortable—but it must be granted that they have not substantially increased the proportionate number of observant Jews even by their less demanding standards.

Yet is there any alternative? Can the scientific, political, aesthetic, philosophic changes of the past century and a half be met with an attitude that seeks mainly to preserve the past? Is timidity in the face of radical change a Jewish virtue? The progressives do not enter upon their roles lightly or proceed capriciously. Theirs is a deeply serious Jewish responsibility which they seek to meet in all its difficulty.

Four intellectual positions may be isolated from the multitude of claims and pronouncements that regularly assault the Jewish community. These are theoretical positions, rarely to be found in Jewish life in abstract and unalloyed form. They cut across most denominational lines as they seek to describe what people believe rather than what label they employ.

One view sees Judaism as a unique religious idea preserved by its similarly unparalleled social carrier. The idea may be termed, too simply, "ethical monotheism," that trust in one real God who undergirds and orders all of creation, but who is distinguished from all other gods of similar mathematical singularity by his righteousness. For the Jew, to know God is first and foremost to be commanded to act ethically, to love one's fellow man, to build a just society. All the wrath and comfort of the prophets, all the planning and exhortation of the rabbis, all the hope and challenge of the messianic idea here come into play. For mankind, despite its pretensions, does not yet understand that this is needed: who God is and what God wants. Jewish distinctiveness is founded in Judaism's conceptual superiority. The Jewish people, as the bearer of the unique idea, as the group which has embodied this belief in their communities in various cultures through the ages, thus has an insight and a unique experience that mankind today needs desperately. Jewish observance, as the means of strengthening and exemplifying this religious truth, is a necessary concomitant of a commitment to this noble historic task. The modern American Jewish community should, by deepening its Jewish roots, devote itself to making justice live, both in its private lives and in general American activity. Then not only the Jews but all mankind will appreciate the worth and value of a continuing Jewish community.

A second view begins from a contrary premise, that there is nothing distinctively Jewish about the idea of one God or the primacy of ethics, or the two taken together. Perhaps in pre-Christian, pre-Moslem, pre-Enlightenment days there was, but today these concepts belong to all thoughtful men. What remains Jewish about the American Jew when his primary concern is ethics, even with a religious grounding, is therefore difficult to see.

Why not rather begin the other way around, with Jews

themselves? They are primarily an ethnic group, and like any other people, have the right to exist and perpetuate their heritage. The individual is inseparable from his people, and the price of turning his back upon it is the insecurity and rootlessness that characterize so many modern Jews. The creation of a flourishing Jewish community begins not with thinking the right ideas but in the personal acceptance of one's Jewishness.

From this decisive sociological step all else flows. Now, Jewish religion follows naturally upon Jewish healthy-mindedness, provided the content of Jewish belief is put in terms modern men can accept. Men want to believe in God; how else could they dream of self-improvement and strive to better their world? Without faith in the universe, they cannot live constructively. When God is thought to be supernatural and otherworldly, the modern mind has no choice but to reject him. With God described instead as a Process or Power working within nature, yet making for human self-fulfillment, scientifically oriented men can accept him. And in consonance with the universality of ethics the concept of the Jews as God's "chosen people" is rejected. The Jews do not now need it to justify their existence, and such a view is incompatible with the brotherhood of mankind. While other ethnic groups take their own way, Jews will naturally articulate their understanding of the one God in their individual folkways as well as be creative in all the other nonreligious forms of folk expression. Thus the Jewish community will grow in continual constructive evolution.

This view has had great appeal to differing groups in the Jewish community. Some culturally oriented Jews have found its primary emphasis upon the Jewish folk a vindication of their view and have been willing to accept the reinterpretation of God that accompanied it as a properly delimited theism. Some traditional Jews, disturbed by the Biblical and prayerbook descriptions of God as a man complete with human emotions and attributes, have found this new view of God liberating. Others, disturbed by the clannishness and self-righteousness of the Jewish community, have been converted by its uncompromising universalism mixed with love of the Jewish people and its culture.

The position has not, however, evoked more than modest enthusiasm. Though it has for thirty years been passionately championed among the leaders of the various Jewish professions, it remains peripheral though alive. Its basic social theory has all the virtues and defects of the protomodern sociology which is its foundation. The American Jew does not find it easy to think of himself primarily as a member of a folk, with his cultural center in the Land of Israel, and only then involved in a particular way of expressing universal religious faith in the United States. The theological suggestions have also faced serious challenge. Religious devotion is either taken deeply or is meaningless, and most men find it difficult if not impossible to become personally involved with a God who is impersonal to them. Moreover, if Jewish commandments are to be thought of as folkways, why should not today's general nonobservance receive sanction and the vulgarity that characterizes much of the folk level of American Jewish life soon become a commandment?

This question of the standards of Jewish life, particularly as they relate to the highest and best in Jewish law, has produced a third view. The Jewish legal tradition, it holds, has ordered and motivated the life of the Jewish people through the ages. Rules of observance both ethical and ritual, not social theories or creeds on the nature of God, have given Jews their distinct character through the ages. Today, when Jews have largely sacrificed Jewish practice for American attainment, to scrap Jewish law would be treason against the generations who held the law sacred, who lived by it and died for it and thus rendered it indispensable. It would also be profitless appeasement of a self-indulgent generation which, in truth, desperately requires the discipline which the law alone can supply.

Not that the present state of traditional Jewish law can speak to modern man. Unfortunately, times have changed more radically than the traditional interpreters of the law could appreciate or accommodate. But the law is not without its inner resources to meet even these unprecedented demands. What is required today is the courage to utilize those special means by which in former times of stress the Jewish sages managed to keep the law true to itself but relevant to its social situation. Such a renaissance of Jewish law must be left to those who are steeped in its ethos, committed to its observance, and thoroughly competent in its sources and methods. Such scholars could produce a body of traditional yet modern Jewish jurisprudence to guide American Jewish life in an authentic way. While their decisions would not bind those who did not wish to accept them, many American Jews would welcome the opportunity to live under a modern Jewish law.

Opponents of this view consider it unworkable in practice and ungrounded in theory. The view has been discussed for decades now, and considerable effort has been made to put it into action with meager results. Few major questions have been treated, and several of these have ended with half the authorities remaining strictly traditional, the rest advocating a position akin to what many in the community had already reached by their private sense of Jewish responsibility. This reticence and indecisiveness have not commended the process to the skeptical observer, but have, rather, raised questions about the realism of the proposal.

Another species of criticism questions the justification of Jewish law today. True, it was central to Judaism in previous ages, but that was because God had revealed and still authorized it. Who or what authorizes Jewish law today? Previous usage surely cannot, for the same theory which proclaims its significance also admits that it is not altogether satisfactory, that in its present state it must be changed to have contemporary relevance. Only the Orthodox can use the argument of previous use, for they intend to continue to use it as it has come down to them. Those who admit the law must be changed must likewise admit the possibility that perhaps its previous indispensability is now moot.

A fourth view focuses on the question of the source of Jewish law, custom, and community—the relationship between God and the people of Israel. Tradition called this the Covenant, and from Biblical days understood it to mean that the one God of the universe was using the Jews in a unique way to carry out his purpose in history. The Covenant exists to bring the Messianic Era, to create and await the Kingdom of God. This is not to deny that the Jews are an ethnic group, but Jewish peoplehood now takes its special meaning in terms of that ancient but continuing pact with God. That is why the character and history of the Jewish people through the ages took a form unparalleled in the records of other peoples or faiths. This people without its God is but a shadow of its historic self and destiny.

Jewish law then is more than ethics or folkways. It is the response of the Jewish people through its prophets and sages to the demands of the real God whom it encountered in history and sought to serve in communal and individual existence. Thus, to speak either of God or the Jewish people or the law alone as the foundation of modern Jewish life is necessarily to minimize the other factors. Only when all are seen in a living relationship does each emerge with full traditional stature. Were the American Jew consciously and voluntarily able to take up that ancient Covenant and make it the mainspring of his life, his observance of its law as a member of its folk would once again be mandated out of his personal relation to God.

This view is relatively new among American Jewry, though it has antecedents in German Jewish thought. One of its strengths is the way in which it cuts across current divisions in the community. By making fundamental the relationship between God and the Jews from which the law emerges, this concept identifies that which all Jews have in common, the relationship. That on which they differ, its implementation in law, is secondary if critical. Moreover, it clarifies what has been permanent in Judaism. The ideas and the language of Jews change from generation to generation; the truth of the Covenant relationship remains forever beyond full articulation, though the life of the Jewish community in history is its clearest human expression.

The sweep of this view is equaled by the problems it engenders. Expressing its unqualified faith in God, it must somehow explain to the quietly agnostic American Jew that God is truly real, a task that modern philosophy and theology make hazardous. To affirm faith in the people, Israel's Covenant with God requires explaining what this can mean in a modern view of history and why Jewish suffering and martyrdom are required in this service. It must also indicate how belief in the Covenant can generate an authentic if modern Jewish way of life. The position has yet to prove itself.

Yet for the Jew who wants to know why his people must continue and what it must do, this view (in agreement with Orthodoxy) unequivocally affirms: God needs Jews. He still uses Jews for his purposes, and they should continue to work and wait for him.

Any of these religious views might produce a vibrant and memorable Jewish life on this continent. But all are subject to the objection raised earlier. Jews, like most mid-century Americans, are timid in faith; they prefer their religion diluted, dispassionate, domesticated. To expect the kind of belief from them by which they will live their whole lives, by which they will restructure their communities, and by whose light they will judge their activities in every economic, political, and social arena is unrealistic. Jews may become synagogue members but not saints. The sociologist with his statistics would scientifically corroborate the present lack of Jewish devotion and the growing social tides working for the dissolution of such Jewishness as remains. Despite the few modest constructive signs noted, the point of no return for American Judaism may already have been passed.

Most American Jews feel this tough-minded truth in their bones. Here arises the pessimism that permeates much sober Jewish self-reflection. At its worst, the mood leads either to the irresponsibility of despair or to the organization man's optimistic fantasy based on his newest program or budget proposal. At its best, Jewish pessimism can make the Jew recognize how hard he must work and what he may realistically expect to accomplish.

That cannot be the final word. What is as unrealistic as Jewish history, as unlikely as Jewish survival and creativity? Yet the Jews have lived; more, they have lived in holiness. Were the Jews of previous ages to have taken a dispassionate, objective view of their future, they too would have despaired. If hardheaded social realism is the only view the modern Jew can bring to his Jewishness, then he will never surmount his pessimism, for Jewish hope was and is founded on Jewish faith. The Jew knows that God keeps the Jewish people alive. He is the Master of their destiny even as he is the Lord of sociology, economics, politics, time, and change. His providence guides human history surely though inscrutably. His help is the source of Jewish strength, and his support the ultimate basis of Jewish dedication. For if this is a stubborn people, he is its equally patient, long-suffering, faithful God. Through and despite political upheaval, economic change, social revolution, cultural evolution, he has kept this people alive. For a Jew, the only true realism is faith in God and commitment to his service. With him Jewish history begins and through him it continues. He alone knows when the end of days shall come and all men will see this great service fulfilled, vindicated, and triumphant.

Jewish theology is the effort to set forth this hopeful faith in self-conscious, intellectual form. It is founded on the equal optimism that such a cognitive effort will help the believing Jew to be more steadfast in his faith and practice, and make it possible for the marginal if not the alienated Jew to reclaim in personal discovery and fulfillment his religious heritage.

2

DEFINITION BY NEGATION: AGAINST THE SECULARIZED SYNAGOGUE

THE CHRISTIAN, particularly the Protestant, often thinks of religion as the ability to affirm a creed as well as the life, individual and communal, which flows from this faith. But for the Jew, religion cannot be so easily identified with the affirmation of a given content of belief, and consequently, the distinction between the secular and the religious—which is so basic to traditional Christian thought—has never been strictly applicable to Judaism. The Jews were a people in the simple ethnic sense of that term before they met their God at Sinai, and the maintenance of that peoplehood has been critical to them in all the centuries that have followed. If Mordecai Kaplan has performed any lasting service in Jewish theology, it is his emphasis on this ethnic component as the inescapable base of all Jewish religiosity and his insistence that a Judaism which knows only God, but not Israel, his people, is no authentic link in the tradition. Indeed, Kaplan's therapy for the ills of contemporary religious life is a thoroughgoing revival of the sense of Jewish peoplehood and its expression in every cultural dimension. The natural result of a healthy Jewishness, he feels, would be a rebirth of Jewish piety in appropriately modern terms.

In one form or other, this diagnosis has become an accepted axiom in responsible American Jewish theology. To proclaim one's faith in God may—so most Jewish thinkers today would agree—yield a general religiosity, but Judaism is reached only when one is equally ready to affirm one's special relation to the Jewish people.

This proposition, however, has had an interesting underground history which is only now beginning to bear fruit. From the very start, the emphasis on the concept of peoplehood has served the needs of those who wanted to be Jewish but could not think of themselves as religious—either because they did not believe in God or (more frequently) because they were anxious to be rid of the discipline of traditional Jewish observance and its European or immigrant overtones. With the help of this folk theory or some variation of it, such nonbelieving or nonobservant Jews (lay and rabbinic alike) could nevertheless devote themselves in all good conscience to Jewish life in its new American style, and they could feel that they were making a contribution to the maintenance and growth of Jewish culture without any commitment to theology or commandments. These would eventually come of themselves or not. In either case, the present would have its rationale.

Now, whatever else may be said of this position, it most certainly involves a distortion of Mordecai Kaplan's view. He has never divided Jewish existence into two separate realms, that of the folk and that of the faith. He has never sought to introduce the categories secular and religious into Judaism in a way that would cut the one aspect off from the other. What he has done is to develop a theory of Jewish existence according to which the people, the social reality, has always had priority over its theology, and he has built a program for the people's future on the basis of this order of value. At the same time he has always insisted that a people's most significant cultural achievement is its religion and that true fulfillment can come to a people only as its religion suffuses its culture. Kaplan has not been unmindful of the dangers posed by those who would use him to set up a fundamental distinction between Jewishness and Jewish religiosity.

Although the secularity of the average synagogue member

in America cannot be understood without reference to this ideological background, he himself is unaware of the sources of his attitudes. He comes, in increasing numbers, to join the synagogue because there are few if any socially acceptable alternatives to synagogue affiliation for one who wants to maintain his Jewish identity and wants his children to be Jewish, in some sense, after him. Though this is not the only motive or level of concern to be found within the synagogue today, the Jew who does not rise above such folk-feeling unquestionably and increasingly represents the synagogue's majority mood. More than that, however, it must be said that he also represents the synagogue's greatest threat. The damaging effect he has already had on the synagogue requires little new description. His newfound affluence and his need for status within the community have made the big building with the small sanctuary, the lavish wedding with the short ceremony, and the fabulous Bar Mitzvah celebration with the minimal religious significance well-established patterns among American Jewish folkways. What other religious group in America can boast of men who are zealously committed to interfaith activities, but who have no faith of their own, who worship in no church with any degree of regularity, and who observe no commandments but those that their organizational participation requires or common American decency decrees? What does it say of Jewish life in America when Reform Judaism appeals because it demands so little but confers so much status? when people blandly proclaim that they are nonobservant Orthodox Jews? when Conservative Judaism makes a virtue of not defining the center so that it may avoid alienating those disaffected on either side?

In short, the secularism that is endemic to the church is reaching into the synagogue as well. But there is a difference, for in the synagogue it claims to be there as of right, as a legitimate interpretation of Jewishness. The church can protect itself from the invasions of secularism by returning to its roots in faith, by a theological analysis of what makes it a church and who therefore has a right to participate in it. And, indeed, such a refining return to theology is today well under way in most of the major Protestant groups.

The impact of this concern with theology is only just beginning to be felt in Protestant life, and it may well be overwhelmed by the secular tides running through the churches. Nevertheless, a significant if small leadership has found the courage to face the issue and striven to meet it, knowing that even if it proves impossible to divert the massive social energies of our day, it may still be possible to prepare the church within the church that will somehow enable the truth of the gospel to survive.

Nothing like this movement in extent or depth is yet to be found in the synagogue. The stirrings of an interest in Jewish theology still affect only a few individuals responding mainly to one another and are limited to that small group within the synagogue who have begun to ask what they really believe.

The leadership of what is purportedly the Jewish religious community is, as a whole, uninterested in theology and is convinced that theology has nothing to do with truly practical questions such as the goals of the community's activity, the methods that are appropriate for reaching them, or the criteria by which either might be judged. If anything, rabbis and laymen alike have a positive antipathy to Jewish theology which among the more articulate and knowledgeable has congealed into an ideology. Judaism, they claim, has never had a theology. It is a religion of deed, not creed. To aspire toward the development of a theology is to assimilate a Christian concern, to impose on Judaism a perspective decidedly uncongenial to it —in other words, it is an attempt to translate Jewish experience into a language appropriate only to Christianity. Moreover, there are practical risks to the theological enterprise. Let a Jewish theology arise and the next step would be to seek conformity to it, to force it upon others and thus destroy that productive pluralism, that creative intellectual dialectic which has been so precious a Jewish privilege.

At the lowest level this view amounts to an elaborate defense of the accomplishments of Jewish organizations, both lay and religious, over the past decade. The varieties of Jewish officialdom may be uneasy over the superficiality of Jewish affiliation and concerned about the meaningful continuity of Jewish life, but not to the extent of encouraging a challenge to the assumptions that underlie the mood of achievement that suffuses the organizational world of American Jewry. Only that theology is welcome which can be harnessed to organizational ends and apparatus, which is an ally and an aid to further institutionalization. No welcome is extended to a radical opposition—even an opposition that exists for the sake of heaven.

The most respectable rejection of Jewish theology stems from a concern for Jewish uniqueness, for the ethnic base of Jewishness and for its survival in some authentic fashion. Spokesmen for this view know Jewish theology only as an effort to establish the universalism of Judaism, to indicate what Jews have believed that all men might find true. Thus to them, theology inevitably involves a sacrifice of the Jewish people, of its specific historic experience and of its present separate existence. Yet whatever the motives behind it, this position, by restraining the religious explication of what is involved in Jewishness—another way of saying Jewish theology—is serving as a major if unwitting instrument in the secularization of Judaism and the synagogue. And in any case, the fear of losing the particularity of Jewish experience is groundless, for under the influence of existentialism, contemporary theology (Christian as well as Jewish) has made its very starting point the particular and concrete existence, in which alone all universals are to be seen and find their meaning; this, indeed, is one of the things that distinguishes it most sharply from the rationalist line of nineteenth-century Jewish thought which was to some extent guilty of sacrificing the idea of Jewish peoplehood to the dream of a universal Judaism.

"Inconsistent" is too mild a word; *chutzpah* alone is adequate to characterize the assertion that theology has no place in Judaism. Because Judaism is basically ethnic, it does not follow that all else in Judaism is optional. What traditional Jewish warrant can be found for the view that Jewish peoplehood is separable from Jewish religiosity? It is only in the last seventy-five years that the idea of Jewishness as a species of secular existence has become so much as conceivable. Judaism has throughout its history asserted that to be a member of the Jewish people was to participate in the Covenant with God and that to partake of Jewish ethnicity was simultaneously to serve God's purpose in history. Modern scholarship has by dint of much diligent toil sought to describe the Jews as they were before Sinai, to picture them as another sub-Semitic group or economic class. But the most important fact about pre-Sinaitic Israel is its utter rejection by classical Jewish literature. Once the secular Hebrews found themselves the people of the Covenant, they knew their only significant origins to be the meetings with God by Abraham and at Sinai. Once the Hebrews had found their new and altered character as God's people, once they had passed beyond the ethnicity of the Hivites, the Jebusites, the Girgashites, their role as the servant-folk of God was all that mattered. Those, then, who consciously or unconsciously are turning the synagogue into an effectively secular institution are blaspheming a sacred history of millennia, indeed, all the history the Jewish people has ever cared to remember until recent years.

But if Jewishness, while ethnic, has a religious component, modern man is entitled to know what Jewish belief means today. Perhaps in an earlier period one could have relied on the solidarity of the Jewish community or the continuity of Jewish practice to bring Judaism safely through the danger of secular domination. But it is precisely the Jewish masses who are the source of the growing secularism, while the standards of Jewish practice have by their continual decline shown their lack of independent foundation or authority. If keeping *kosher* were still regarded as God's command, the Jew might well withstand the many-layered temptations that arise to violate it. If study were a *mitzvah* and not another possibility for leisure-time recreation, then Jewish learning might be a thick hedge surrounding the remnants of Jewish piety. But since neither the spirit nor the practice of "catholic Israel" suffices any longer to assure meaningful Jewish continuity, Jews are all the more in need of an adequate statement of Jewish faith relevant to this day, for only such faith can restore the Jewish community to its goals and to the duties they entail. Where another generation might seek to meet its problems by trusting naïvely to the onward motion of an unfolding organic development, Jews today are deprived of any such trust. History and sociology have shown them where they have been and where they are tending—shall they now pretend that they are blind? They have all the sophistication that self-knowledge and self-consciousness confer—where shall they hope to find the innocence of ignorance? Secularism is rising in religious guise, powered by the social and economic readjustments of a postimmigration, postdepression, and postwar America. To hide from this knowledge is simultaneously to spurn our freedom, and by preferring illusion to reality, to contemn the franchise of modernity. The question can no longer be whether Jewishness has always had a religious content or whether one really need discuss it. The only honest question left to ask is, How shall one speak of Jewish faith?

True, such efforts cannot hope to speak out of an unbroken tradition of theology which has grown and developed with Judaism itself. For many reasons, the philosophic explication of faith has not, in the past, seemed a necessary part of Israel's continuing intellectual activity. Thus, to develop a Jewish theology today, to explain what would purport to be an authentic Judaism, inevitably means using concepts and standards devised in a Christian context for Christian purposes. Such a task of translation seems forbiddingly formidable. Yet similar labor has been done before in Jewish Diaspora experience. Indeed, the classic expressions of Jewish theological creativity were the products of a cross-fertilization of Judaism and some other culture. The incursion of Hellenistic thought into Judaism, for example, made Philo both possible and necessary. And Maimonides was compelled to write the *Guide for the Perplexed* (and, one might argue, even his *Code*) because in his time Judaism was challenged by an Islam confident of its own truth and able to argue for itself in Neo-Aristotelian terms. Neither Philo nor Maimonides nor any of their colleagues had a traditionally Jewish yet "universal" theological vocabulary to draw upon. They had to fashion one out of the general philosophic material of their day—and they succeeded in doing so without surrendering their Judaism. They succeeded because they did their borrowing in all Jewish self-respect, limiting their acquisitions to what they felt were the limits set by their Jewish faith, and transforming what they had borrowed to suit their Jewish goals. Philo's *logos* is qualitatively distinct from that of his Hellenistic predecessors, and Maimonides, who knows Aristotle's thesis of the eternity of matter so well that he can on its account break with the Moslem philosophic tradition of proving God from creation, will not surrender completely to that thesis because it might imperil Judaism's insistence upon miracle and freedom. If Jewish theology must always be an "answering" theology, then the risk of falsifying Judaism will always have to be run. Still, there is ample Jewish precedent to show that the risks can be overcome and that Judaism can thereby acquire a new vitality. If anything, the fact that Christianity stems from Judaism and seeks indigenously to relate to Judaism's God makes it at once easier and more necessary to find a means of saying, in language both can share, where the two must differ and where they must agree.

Such a quest for intellectual clarity need not restrict Judaism's traditional freedom in the realm of thought. There is a significant difference between dogmatic and systematic theology. The former is an effort to clarify and explain, perhaps even to justify, what a member of a church with dogmas must believe. The latter also seeks to clarify, explain, and justify faith, but if the church does not insist on defining the content held necessary for membership, then the theology may, at best, come to be pervasive, accepted, and universally relied upon. The sense of discipline or obligation need not appear.

Judaism could hardly tolerate a dogmatic theology, for dogma, taken strictly, is alien to its spirit and experience. Rigor and authority are known only in the realm of Jewish practice, of halachah, but have rarely been introduced into the realm of thought. Thus, the closest thing to a dogmatic theology in Judaism might once have been a theology of the halachah. But with authority in the area of Jewish practice as eroded as it has become, such an enterprise, even were it able to surmount the almost insuperable academic difficulties involved, would still only be as coercive as its argument was persuasive.

Inhospitality to dogmatic theology, however, still leaves ample room for the systematic theology that would seek to set forth the content of Jewish belief in an integrated and reasoned way. The authority of such a theology would rest on its ability to convince, not on its special ecclesiastical status, and its very presence in the intellectual forum would require those with other views, or none, to meet its arguments and match its standards.

Since Jewish theology must be systematic rather than dogmatic, a reawakening of theological concern might very well result in a variety of views and approaches. But so far as the fight against the new religiosecularism is concerned, this would make very little difference, and so far as Judaism is concerned, it would be all to the good. Such disagreements could be resolved in meaningful and constructive debate, and if not resolved, they would at least contribute to the clarification of alternative possibilities in Jewish faith—while showing, incidentally, how baseless is the fear that the development of a modern Jewish theology will lead to creedal compulsion. For most modern views, freedom of conscience is the very foundation of thought and their concern with theology stems in the first place from their desire to transform Judaism from a social fate into a free commitment of conscience.

What Judaism needs, then, is not a theology, but theological concern, not theological uniformity but theological informedness. Whether expressed in a single pattern or in several patterns, this would make possible the corrected vision required—sharp focus on the religious component of Jewishness.

It would, of course, be naïve to suppose that mere intellectual formulation and discussion could have an immediate or powerful effect on a community as ethnically rooted and as happily integrating as American Jewry. Still, every man of intellectual self-respect would feel himself challenged, and the new, biting quality to the quest for a meaningful Jewish identity would influence many. Through serious theological discussion Jewish identity would be defined, Jewish commitments and obligations outlined. Anyone who had the willingness to do so would finally be given an opportunity to direct his Jewish interest to serious Jewish living, and those who were still standing indecisively at the margins of the congregation would be provided with an incentive to join the community of the faithful. Perhaps a decisive minority could be won.

The positive hope is obvious—but there might also be a negative consequence from which one must not shy away. Clarifying Jewish faith might bring many to the conclusion that they cannot honestly participate in Judaism and the synagogue. Jewish theology could thus become a means of driving Jews from the synagogue. No one wishes to lose Jews for Judaism, but the time has come when the synagogue must be saved for the religious Jew, when it must be prepared to let some Jews opt out so that those who remain in, or who come in, will not be diverted from their duty to God. As the religion of a perpetual minority, Judaism must always first be concerned with the saving remnant, and so long as the synagogue is overwhelmed by the indifferent and the apathetic who control it for their own nonreligious purposes, that remnant will continue to be deprived of its proper communal home. By defining the issues, clarifying the goals, challenging the conventions, Jewish theology may help save a faithful seed and thus round out its prophetic function in our time.

Would there, then, be no place in this community for the secular Jew? Would he be excommunicated, cut off forever from the Jewish people? Surely the answer must depend upon the secularist's own Jewish concern. Some secular Jews have no interest in the Jewish people at all. They are Jews by birth and their secularism, they say, is purely human and universal, neither having nor requiring any particular foundation (which prompts the obvious comment that, remarkably, this urban, intellectual, universal type is a Jew). The responsibility of the religious community to such Jews would be to help them see what Judaism is and might be. But their right (and perhaps their duty) to stop being known as Jews would be all the more available to them as a matter of free choice.

The Jew who is secular in the sense of lacking religious faith but loyal to the Jewish community—the man who wants neither God nor commandments, but who likes Jews, the Jewish approach to life, or the Jewish style of being different—is the more difficult problem, perhaps because he is so new to the Jewish scene. What would an adequate Jewish theology say to him? Concerned with Jewish peoplehood and Jewish history, it would somehow have to come to terms with all the various groupings into which this people has evolved, and with all the transitional forms in which so many of them find themselves—though it would also have to judge the ultimate value of these groupings and forms in terms of their relation to God. Committed to *Klal Yisrael,* to all of Jewry as well as to God, the new Jewish theology would probably take an ambivalent attitude to the committed Jewish secularist. He has a place among his people as long as he wishes one—nevertheless he does not stand within its traditional frame. He has his rights as worker, seeker, contributor—but hardly as leader, spokesman, or exemplar. He must be called "Jew," for there is no other useful term for him—nevertheless he is not, in his rejection of the Jewish faith, a "true," a "real," a "good" Jew. So long as his Jewish loyalty is limited to the people but not to the God it serves, he must be considered truncated and unfulfilled.

Jewish theology, therefore, has a special responsibility to him, both as challenge and alternative. It must ask him the source of his values, the foundations of his beliefs, in people, in ideals, in Jewishness itself. It must help him reach the profound questions of human existence to which Judaism has been a response. And over against his own implicit faith, it must pose the faith of the Jewish ages, now interpreted fresh and anew. It must help him face the need to believe, which is basic to any life of ideals, and it must then help him build a personal foundation in faith that can reach up to all men and the whole of human history. Within this context it must set before him in cogent fashion the riches, the depth, the maturity in value which centuries of experience in many different worlds of culture have brought to Judaism. How many intellectuals there are who know everything there is to know about minor novelists and poets and painters, but dismiss as insignificant a Judaism they stopped studying at the age of thirteen! Such Jews, too, should feel free—perhaps they should even be encouraged—to leave a Jewish people they discover irrevocably wed to God. But the Jewish theologian affirms his vocation as an affirmation of Judaism, in the faith that Judaism can only benefit from exposition and scrutiny. He trusts that he may communicate not concepts alone, but faith, and that he may arouse not understanding alone, but commitment.

3

DEFINITION BY NEGATION: AGAINST CHRISTIAN NEO-ORTHODOXY

TWENTY YEARS have passed since Irving Kristol, in a savage critique of Milton Steinberg's book *Basic Judaism,* sought to demonstrate that Jewish thought in America was powerless to answer the great questions—questions about man and his condition, about destiny and the meaning of history—that the war had raised in the troubled minds of so many intellectuals in the West. Kristol's article challenged Jewish thinkers to face these questions instead of taking refuge in the kind of calm, confident faith that he accused Milton Steinberg, and most American rabbis, of preaching. To this challenge a group of younger theologians—among them Emil L. Fackenheim and Will Herberg—soon responded, and for a time it seemed that a new Jewish theology—a theology concerned with the crisis of the age—was in process of being born. But the effort miscarried. Aside from a few articles and one book, perhaps two, the promise of these first few exciting efforts remained unfulfilled.

Now that two decades have passed, it is helpful to ask why this new Jewish theology failed to develop. To do so, one must return to Kristol's argument and set forth its basic thesis. What disturbed him was the relative indifference of American Judaism to the extent and complexity of the problem of sin. He wrote that "the spiritual distress of the modern world does not arise merely because man perversely chooses to do evil rather than good. If it were as uncomplicated as all that, present-day Judaism—even Rabbi Steinberg's Judaism—would have the answer right at hand. The horror that breathes into our faces is the realization that evil may come by doing good —not merely *intending* to do good, but *doing* it."

Jewish theology to be meaningful in the postwar world would have to speak to this problem—to man's talent for creating evil, to his capacity for deluding himself about the strength and subtlety of his evil inclination. Contemporary Jewish thinkers, of whom Steinberg was then the most articulate, lacked the courage or the vision to see the problem, much less to provide the answers. Books, journals, and sermons seemed quite satisfied with the liberal formulas and melioristic illusions of the thirties. To read or hear them was to experience the eerie feeling that their authors had been suspended in time or that in their limited vision they had remained oblivious to what meanwhile had happened to mankind. Thus for men such as Irving Kristol who were preoccupied with the ordeal of Western culture, a Judaism without an emphasis on the problem of sin was "still catastrophically narrow," and was characterized by "intellectual timidity, cultural immaturity." So went the appraisal and the challenge.

It is not difficult to recall the circumstances which engendered this troubled concern with religion and with its failure to take sufficient account of the realities of human evil. By 1948, the mood of which Kristol's article was only one of many expressions was already prominent in American Protestant circles which were experiencing the same disillusionment that their European colleagues had learned a war earlier. A few years before, everything had seemed so clear. The professors had swept out the dead dogmas of tradition and had confidently pointed the way to a better world. The politicians, particularly the radicals, had been even more convinced that their revelation was truth. Political action, scientific investigation, man for himself—such notions became the messianic hopes, the pseudoreligions, which were shattered by the realities of World War II and the cold war that succeeded it. Once these new idols had been discredited by the tragic complexities of what was now seen to be the human condition, religion itself began to appear in a new role and to take on new meaning. If man could not play God successfully, then perhaps God himself was not dead. If man could not finally stand in effective judgment over his own pride and sinfulness, then God could and would—perhaps, indeed, had. To rebuild his life, to be true to his new view of history, postwar man needed to understand not only his limitations but also his profound capacity for evil even in the guise of doing good. With their continuing revelations of both democratic and communist deceit and treachery, the years since World War II have only made the problem more pressingly relevant. As a result, the theology of sin—and related to it, the theology of the state and its functions, the theology of culture and of history—have continued to be central concerns of Western thought.

The impact of this vast change was felt with special power in the Jewish world, for the thirties had had a special significance for American Jews. They were the first years of rapid integration into American culture. Out of the ghetto neighborhoods had come great numbers of young adults intent on becoming true Americans and on making use of a freedom that had been won after long centuries of persecution. Their Jewish heritage, with its emphasis on intellect and self-assertion, also made the American opportunities for education and advancement particularly attractive. No liberal, scientific, or cultural movement was without its youthful Jewish zealots. No group should therefore have been more disillusioned by the experiences of the forties or have been more attuned to the appeal made by Kristol's article.

Yet the record of the succeeding years is clear. The prevalent mood of the Jewish community since World War II has not been one of concern with human sinfulness or with man's inability to transcend evil. It has not been characterized by resignation or despair. On the contrary, though the American Jew may be politically less naïve, even to the point of near apathy, and though he may not be as trusting as he once was of those who have simple solutions for our society's ills, the dominant accent of his life is still his faith in the Good Deed.

Indeed, what stands out in a review of the life of American Jews during the fifties is not a mood of indecision or even hesitation, but a clear and simple knowledge of what they needed to do—and then did. Marriage, children, decent jobs, and homes—these often led them to new neighborhoods or to communities which had not existed a few years before. There were no established institutions, no patterns of community life, waiting to receive them. Still, even in the presence of communal nothingness they knew what needed to be done. There must be Jewish schools for Jewish children, Jewish centers for Jewish youth, synagogues and temples for—of all people—them! There must be organized Jewish communities, if for no other reason than that they might work together to rescue brother Jews from refugee camps, from lands of oppression, or wherever they were in distress. And American Jews did what they could, from sending telegrams to running rummage sales, from attending mass meetings to offering quiet prayers to create, build, and maintain the State of Israel. It was not the Jewish professionals or the great national organizations which developed this attitude—though even they often take credit for it. Their role, however significant, was shaped in response to a process that was already under way in the Jewish community. In short, without ever having to think about it, the masses of American Jewry emerged from World War II not with a sense of man's helplessness before the evil consequences of his well-intentioned behavior or of the powerlessness of his will before his own evil inclinations, but rather with what can legitimately be called an irreplaceable faith in man's capacity to know the righteous act and accomplish it successfully.

To be sure, one may condemn much of what American Jews have done in the past decade as merely the exuberant response of those newly admitted into the suburban middle class. Yet it seems fair to say that it is not mere middle-class morality but a history of commitment to the concept of *mitzvah*, commandment, which has asserted itself in contemporary American Jewish life. *Chupah v'kiddushin, pru ur'vu, talmud torah, tzedakah*—"marriage," "procreation," "education," "charity"—these and a hundred other commandments may be unacknowledged as such by the American Jew, but they still guide his life. He does not, of course, study the codes of Jewish law as his great-grandfather did, and he may even believe that they no longer have relevance. Nevertheless, it seems clear that centuries of Jewish devotion and observance have conditioned his psyche so thoroughly that virtually no amount of rebellion, flight, and camouflage has been able to purge him of the conviction that a man is capable both of knowing and doing the good. This conviction—which forms the very basis of Judaism and which is one of the main points on which Christianity split from its mother religion—has continued to dominate the life of American Jewry in our day, despite wars, crises, and intellectual disillusion.

Starting with that faith—obscure though it may be—the ordinary American Jew has raised his own theological questions. Though he may not practice such commandments as he does out of any conscious religious commitment, still the acts themselves lead him to inquiries about their origin, purpose, and authority. From within the Jewish community, from Jewish living and devotion, there has thus arisen a distinct and indigenous desire for theology—only this is for a theology of *mitzvah*, a rationale of the Jewish way of life and belief. Thus, first by the witness of its life and then by the questions which that life poses, American Jewry has in effect rejected the kind of question raised in Irving Kristol's article.

This is not to say that the problem of sin has disappeared from Jewish *intellectual* life. Along with the related questions of culture, the state, and history, it still comes before the handful of thinkers who take the discipline of theology seriously. Yet to expound a Jewish theology relevant to our day, one must decide whether to begin with the problem of sin or the value of *mitzvah.* In the one case, man's continued failure is taken as the basis of religious experience. In the other case, the need and the ability to do the righteous act become the concern in thought that they have previously been in life.

Contemporary Jewish thought in America, confronted by these two paths of theology, has chosen the latter, the one which has always been characteristic of Judaism. Traditionally, it is Christianity that has been most preoccupied with the problem of sin, for to Christianity the most basic and overwhelming fact of human existence is man's sinfulness before God's law. Man, said Paul, cannot perform the commandments, though he exert himself to the fullest. Because man's will is corrupt, the Torah is inherently self-defeating: if anything, God's purpose in giving it was to prove that it was impossible to reach him through merit. Salvation can only come to the unworthy sinner through God's grace, and even after the sinner has been redeemed, he continues to be dependent on divine grace for living the good life. In Christianity, then, first comes the theology of sin, then the theology of redemption, and finally the theology of justification and sanctification (the theology of righteous living).

Judaism has traditionally faced life from a different point of view. What has amazed the Jew, leaving him in awe and trembling, is his declared ability to know and to do a righteous act. That he, an ant, a grasshopper, is privileged to know God's will and to perform it, that he, a mote in the vastness of creation, is still by reason of this knowledge and this capacity "but little lower than God" (the Hebrew says *elohim*)—this has been the primary source of his religious inspiration. His Bible is filled not with philosophic disquisitions, with metaphysical analyses, but with laws and commandments, histories of how he lived under this regimen, and prophetic harangues that criticize his performance and refine his responsibilities. The vast libraries of rabbinic literature are not filled with guides to religious introspection but, rather, seek to make ever clearer the details of the religiously responsible act. Even the medieval philosophers discuss the existence and attributes of God primarily as a basis for validating and authorizing the life of Torah.

Judaism knows sin and sinfulness, but understands them within the context of *mitzvah*, not vice versa. When the Jew sins, he is not overwhelmed by the event, nor does he anticipate that God will be. The Jew knows that he is but an animal. Surely, this cannot come as a surprise to God, his creator, who fashioned him of dust. Hence, God will understand the lapse; and because what he wants, more than punishment, is the righteous act, he will allow man to turn from his evil and pursue righteousness again. Even in his sinfulness, the Jew does not simply wait for God to act. Even then, there is a *mitzvah* to perform. The Jew acts. He does *teshuvah:* he turns his life to righteous living with an immediate act of repentance, and he knows his heartfelt turning to his Maker will be accepted.

Thus it is not especially difficult to understand why the demand for a new Jewish theology, the Jewish theology of man's sinfulness, has had little effect. Instead, there has been another concern, a concern that arose from within the Jewish community, based upon its commitments, and one that Judaism has always considered more elementary. To this theology of *mitzvah*, Jewish thinkers, particularly the younger ones, have increasingly given their attention. It is symptomatic that the articles by Emil Fackenheim in the past decade have moved from the consideration of human limitations to the possibility in liberal Judaism for authoritative guidance of Jewish living. Fackenheim's intellectual odyssey is similar to that of most postwar Jewish theologians.

It would be premature to call this effort to articulate a theology of *mitzvah* a distinct school of thought. At the moment there is no book, personality, nor institution around which it might be organized (though it owes much to the writings of Franz Rosenzweig and Martin Buber). However, it has enlisted the interest of diverse Jewish thinkers and the broad outlines of one emerging style can be sketched. This approach might be called "Covenant Theology," for it rests upon a reaffirmation, in contemporary terms, of the Covenant of Sinai and its renewal during the centuries of prophetic leadership. It seeks to explore and understand the implications of defining religion as a covenant relation, and specifically to make manifest the nature and meaning of the Jewish Covenant with God.

Covenant Theology, then, understands Judaism in frankly existential terms. Judaism involves not only a set of ideas, a concept of God, or even a set of practices; it is also a way of living one's life based on a relationship with God, a relationship in which the whole self is involved. But it is not simply the private faith of an individual. The Jew is the man who shares in the mutual promise existing between God and Israel —that is, the Jewish people as a whole. The Covenant was not made between one Jew and God, but between God and the entire House of Israel. The individual Jew shares in his people's relationship with God as a matter of birth. He may also share in it as a matter of will when he makes this historic Covenant the chief article of his faith.

The Covenant, begun with Abraham, sealed at Sinai, renewed a dozen times over through the prophets, and reaffirmed by succeeding generations of Jews, thus provides the base for the new theology. Under that Covenant the Jews have acknowledged *Adonai,* "the Lord," alone as God and have pledged themselves to live by his law. Here the new theologians emphasize the *mitzvah,* for it is through this service, individually and communally, that Israel testifies to God's reality, nature, and existence through all of history. Israel will remain faithful to God and his service until all men come to know him, that is, to live by God's law. Israel does not believe that any other religion has been or would be able to carry out that function. Israel believes that God will preserve and protect the Jewish people through all of history—though that care is not extended from the people as a whole to each Jewish family or individual, as contemporary Jews have so bitterly learned. Israel knows that God will vindicate its striving on his behalf on the day when all men indeed do come to know him.

The central task of modern Judaism, according to this theology, is to win the conscious, willed loyalty of the modern Jew to the Covenant. Other generations could take the Jew's acceptance of the Covenant for granted. Yesterday's Jew grew up in a community which lived by it, and it so informed his personal and group life that he did not even have to articulate it. If he had begun to question it, the whole force of his intellectual orientation would have led him to a resolution. Today's Jew does not have the benefit of living and thinking within this pattern. If the Covenant is to bind his children and his children's children, he must come to accept it as his personal Covenant as well. By making it inform his life and the life of his family, by seeing that his children receive a proper Jewish education and by encouraging them to marry within the religion, by living a life of Torah, he must work to ensure that the Covenant will be transmitted to future generations.

In the eyes of the new theology, then, the modern Jew must be not only an ethical man, not only a religious man, but the man of the Covenant as well. He is a Jew because he affirms that Covenant and has made it the basis of his existence. Once he does so, his life becomes an effort to sanctify time, to redeem history through following the commandments, by performing other righteous deeds. Each commandment not only becomes a way to personal improvement and fulfillment, but also helps to satisfy his responsibility to God and to mankind. Similarly, in performing the *mitzvot* he makes his own life more holy and brings the world that much closer to the Kingdom of God. As he becomes more observant, ethically as well as ritually, in his practical life as well as in study and prayer, he not only comes to know his God more intimately but speaks of him to all mankind.

Moreover, the Covenant explains to him that great mystery of which he personally has been a witness and participant—Israel's continuing survival. Only a generation ago, some Jews were calculating how soon American Jewry would disappear. Today the complaint is that education and observance do not go far enough, that Judaism must become more profound. Having suffered the worst calamity the Covenant people has ever known, the House of Israel has responded with new will and determination. No answer can be given to why God demands such suffering from the Jews under the Covenant, yet that neither condones nor minimizes Jewish persecution. The new thinkers do, however, point to the fact that the ties which bind Jews one to another have not been broken by persecution and suffering, but continue to be strengthened in the course of meeting common Jewish problems. The creation of the State of Israel and its continuing survival, they affirm, is also moving evidence that the Covenant continues.

The specific details of what is meant by "God's law" will vary among Jewish groups. They do not differ over the abiding relation between God and Israel, but—as is traditional in Judaism—about Torah: that is, the specific ways through which the Covenant shall be made manifest in life. The Orthodox will insist that traditional Jewish law, subject to change only within carefully circumscribed limits, is the only authentic expression of the relationship. The Conservative will agree that the institution of law must continue but will insist that Jewish law has historically adapted itself to new circumstances, and that it contains within it all the necessary means for defining how one should live under the Covenant and still be part of American society. The reformers will insist on the freedom of the individual to decide questions of ritual observance in terms of his conscience or his personal encounter with the Divine. But just as the other groups will benefit by the emphasis in the new theology on God's role, so the Reform Jew will find that the role of Israel asserts itself deeply in his consciousness. By seeing Judaism as the Covenant faith, he will regard it not as a private religion, but as one he shares with his people. Hence his right to decide what is Torah for him, which might lead to anarchy, will be expanded to what is Torah for him as a member of the Covenant-folk. From the point of view of Covenant Theology, then, what binds Jews together is far more important than what separates them. Their differences, particularly as modified by the role of the *mitzvah* in the lives of families and communities, become far more a matter of degree than of kind.

Understanding Judaism as a Covenant can also explain why modern Jews believe in the continuing worth of righteousness despite the ubiquity of sin. They know that religion always involves two partners, God and man. Jewish history has seen the doleful results of overemphasizing the role of either. The reliance upon God alone in times of oppression and persecution has often acted to reduce the role of *mitzvah,* to relieve the people of its responsibility to use its own powers for justice and peace. And the insistence upon man as the master of history explains the continuing stream of false messiahs and of the spiritual ordeal that inevitably follows their exposure—for example, the prophets of social change and scientism of the thirties, followed by the despair of the forties. It is true that despite man's best efforts the Messianic Era does not arrive. But one need not then conclude that it can never come. God, too, has a share in its coming, and in his own good time, if not our own, that great Messianic Day will dawn. This sure faith that God stands with him in history can give the individual Jew the patience, the holy obstinacy, to endure and to act. God moves through history, working out his will for the creation, and man has the privilege of serving as his partner, though not as his surrogate.

Sin might destroy the Jewish will to act if the Jew believed that sin might destroy the Covenant, that it might nullify the relationship between God and man. But Judaism long ago affirmed that its Covenant was eternal—that is, unconditional. God may punish, exile, decimate Israel. Still the Covenant remains. The prophets may denounce Israel in His name; they may insist that he will render judgment upon it as upon any other sinful nation, and perhaps even more severely—still, they do not say he will revoke his Covenant. Israel's obligations under that continuing Covenant are precisely what call forth the prophetic denunciation and the punishment of God.

The Jews, then, have traditionally rejected Paul's thesis that the Covenant is obsolete and that a new Covenant is required. The living reality of their relation with their God despite their failures, their experience of the response of their God to them in their sin, their trust that he has taken upon himself part of the responsibility of history—all combine to bring them to assert faith in the Covenant despite their inability to fulfill it on their own.

There is much more to be said about both *mitzvah* and sin. Still, in true Jewish fashion it is life which must strengthen and intensify theology so that theology may in turn direct and order life. Only as American Jewry comes to live by the Covenant in a rapidly shifting culture can Jews determine its lasting significance for Judaism. But should that life of the Covenant become real and pervasive—whether in its rationalistic, humanistic, or existentialistic form—the foundation will have been laid for Jewish theology to reach out to the broader questions of culture, of the state, of the history of non-Jewish peoples. Until then the primary task of the Jewish thinker remains within the community of Israel. Some will still find this devotion to be as "catastrophically narrow" as Kristol did twenty years ago. But the Jew, the man who through the Covenant has survived the Hellenistic, Persian, Moorish cultures, and a dozen more—the man who, as it were, has survived the forces of history itself—will but marvel at such myopia. For in reaffirming the Covenant, in making it his own, in reestablishing his people's loyalty to it, the Jew enables himself and his people to transcend geography and politics, civilization and time.

Perhaps the greatest contribution Jews can make to Western culture is simply in living by the Covenant of their fathers, in patiently pursuing righteousness until God's Kingdom comes. Western man reels between the poles of "forcing the end" and despairing of man's power. The people of Israel has in great part learned to avoid both evils. It knows its role in history as it knows God's. That it can affirm such faith in man and God, that it can continue to live by that faith, should be a source of continuing wonder for all mankind, and, hopefully, a spur to similar faith and action.

Part Two

EXAMINING THE THEOLOGICAL OPTIONS

4

LEO BAECK: BEYOND NEO-KANTIANISM

JEWISH THEOLOGY regularly arises in a particular social situation and that determines its distinctive character. Theology is not native to Judaism, for the centuries of its Biblical Talmudic development are essentially free of it. There are traces of argument in the Bible, on rare occasions an extended discussion, and the rabbis use logic to expound the Torah. Nonetheless, they do not know the sort of abstraction and probing that characterize philosophy or theology. (The terms are used here in a loose construction, since the differences between them which so agitate the contemporary discussion were not alive in the time under consideration.) Not until first-century Judaism confronts Hellenistic Greek thought in Alexandria does the first full-scale Jewish philosophy appear; then it is rather quickly ignored by the normative Jewish community. Were it not for the church's preservation of Philo, there would be no record of Jewish theological reflection until the time of the interaction with the flourishing Moslem civilization of the late ninth century. For its first two thousand years, from Moses to Isaac Israeli, Judaism, despite contact with Greek civilization, had little need for philosophic analysis of its faith. Only in the past thousand years, and then only in periods of open cultural intercourse (e.g., in Spain but not in Turkey or Poland) does a self-conscious concern with the intellectual content and character of Jewish faith assert itself. Jewish theology is the product of social hybridization.

The emancipation of European Jewry creates that sort of situation more radically than did Alexandria or Spain, for the modern Jew is far more accepted today than ever before. The Alexandrian Jew was a monotheist among pagans. The Spanish Jew was tolerated but inferior. The modern Jew is in theory and often in practice a person fully equal to all other persons. His continuing Jewish faith may be odd but it is his private right.

What was implicit in all previous Jewish theological effort now comes more clearly to the surface. Two criteria must be met if the enterprise is to succeed. The theology must be cast in a modern form, for it is the modern social situation that calls it forth. Yet the Judaism so conveyed must somehow remain authentic or it does not merit the description "Jewish."

The tension of these demands is already apparent in the first theoretician of modern Jewishness, Moses Mendelssohn. A deep rift runs through his thought, separating belief from observance. In the content of his faith he is fully modern, a classic example of the pre-Kantian enlightenment mentality with its emphasis on the rationality and universality of the human spirit. Yet he also affirms an unparalleled revelation of law at Sinai which is supernatural and particularistic. Jewish practice therefore is fixed within limits that cannot be changed. Mendelssohn is fully modern in belief and fully Jewish in practice. Such a reconciliation of the two demands, as its speedy abandonment by his closest followers shows, cannot be maintained. The need for integrity—perhaps, then, a third criterion—soon makes this unharmonizable two-leveled approach to truth unacceptable.

The thinker's task would be easier if he could know in advance just what acceptable modernity and authentic Judaism are. Determining them turns out to be a substantial part of his labor and his risk. Again the case of Mendelssohn is instructive. His argument for immortality caused a sensation when it was published, yet within a generation it carried no weight with thoughtful readers. Once Kant had published the first of his great critiques, man's thinking about souls and spirit was so revolutionized that Mendelssohn no longer made sense. What was acceptably modern had itself changed. In a way, the problem of an authentic Judaism has also changed since Mendelssohn's time. Later generations of Jews, in overwhelming number, modified his fixed regimen of Jewish observance. They did this in conscious opposition to those Jews who adopted Christianity. They modernized their practice as part of an effort to continue to affirm Judaism. Partly they felt compelled to their reforms as a result of accepting modern criteria of truth and value. Mostly it was an adaptation to the social realities of life outside the ghetto. In any case, they felt intuitively that their new style of living was, despite its departures from the tradition, not untrue to the Jewish past, and an acceptable Jewish theology for them would have to explain that truth. The demand for an authentic Judaism now also means the enunciation of a standard of legitimate change and continued fixity in Judaism. That would identify for the non-Orthodox what they knew in their lives to be their authentic Judaism.

If that defines the project of liberal Jewish theology, it is no wonder that Hermann Cohen may be said to be the first to bring it to fulfillment. The nineteenth century had known distinguished Jewish thinkers, but in Cohen the level of his modernity and the quality of his insight into Judaism reached new and exemplary heights. His work spans the period of Germany's emergence from the Franco-Prussian War of 1870 to World War I, his definitive book on Judaism appearing posthumously in 1919.

There can be no question about Cohen's adequacy as a modern thinker. As a young man he was invited to the University of Marburg to teach philosophy. In only three years and despite his Jewishness, he was appointed full professor, a status far more difficult to attain in the German university system than in the American. Cohen's extraordinary rise to academic eminence was due to his brilliant reconstruction of the Kantian system which after some decades of eclipse by various forms of Hegelianism he and some others now returned to prominence. Cohen's own solution to the problems of the Kantian philosophy was so telling it became the cornerstone of one of the three great patterns of Neo-Kantianism that now emerged, the so-called Marburg school version.

This work was purely secular and academic. It had no inner relationship to the fact of Cohen's Jewish birth and early Jewish education. That is so much the case that tracing the resurgence of Cohen's Jewish sympathies and the eventual development of his religious sentiments has become a standard theme in the Jewish interpretation of his work. What is essential to his credentials as a fully qualified modern thinker is that he achieved his recognition as a secular philosopher, not as an expounder of Judaism. Ironically and significantly, had Cohen not so succeeded in the general culture, his subsequent exposition of Judaism would not have received the Jewish acceptance it did.

Cohen's technical work, resolving the paradoxes inherent in Kantianism, is not relevant here. Yet a word must be said about his thought insofar as it made possible his new philosophy of Judaism. Cohen continued and elaborated the Kantian emphasis on ethics which remains the key to understanding man and organizing society. In the Cohenian exposition it is an eternal task whose accomplishment becomes more realized yet remains infinitely distant. So the duty itself and not its full working out becomes the center of man's existence. Yet that task must be carried out in the real world, for it cannot be left on a conceptual or imaginative level. Nature, however, again in a Kantian sense, is seen as the realm disclosed by science, and that is value free. A disturbing dichotomy suddenly disrupts the rationality of man's universe. The natural and ethical domains must be linked if the ethical task is to be possible. There must also be some guarantee that it can continue forever. That is possible only if the system contains an idea which transcends each realm so as to let it maintain its own structure and individuality, yet is an idea comprehensive enough to bring them into harmonious relationship. There is thus a rational necessity for the idea of God, which asserts primarily the unity and uniqueness of God and his importance to man through His grounding of ethics. For a technical philosopher whose primary concerns were intellectual and academic, not apology for religion, that was an extraordinary and astonishing accomplishment.

It turned out to be well adapted to philosophizing about the nature of Judaism, but Cohen did not turn directly to this task until after his retirement in 1912. Much of what was to follow was already known from Cohen's less systematic work and because, despite his originality, he was the continuation of the nineteenth-century German Jewish effort to explain Judaism in Kantian terms. Yet his lectures of the World War I period, though not a fully systematic presentation of his understanding of Judaism, disclose a sophistication of intellect, a richness of insight, and a depth of sympathy which set a new standard for subsequent Jewish thought.

Cohen's philosophy of Judaism is entitled (see the discussion below) *Religion of Reason Out of the Sources of Judaism.* Reason, that is, philosophy, determines the structure of what an appropriate human religion would be. When one turns to the literary sources of Judaism, one finds this sort of religion incredibly well attested. It is, of course, expressed in ways more natural to prephilosophic man. Yet wherever one looks in Judaism the unity and uniqueness of God are being asserted or safeguarded. Jewish law in all its variety turns out to be an elaborate system for cultivating ethical sensitivity in the most diverse areas of existence where it is not being enjoined directly. Jewish thought and practice anticipated and translated into discipline the modern, rational understanding of God and man. For Cohen, Judaism is the classic representation of religion of reason.

One can thus identify what should remain permanent in Judaism—its ethics and its God. These are its lasting, unique characteristics. Cohen does see the need for ceremony and ritual, that is, the nonethical commandments of the tradition. Against the radical reformers of his time he argued for the retention of the Hebrew language in prayer, study, and other such expressions of historic Judaism. Still, he could not ascribe to any of these acts the same importance he gave to ethical duty. Thus, while the nonethical acts might be valuable or useful, one could not insist that they were unchanging or permanently required. So a criterion of continuity in change had been enunciated.

Defining ethical monotheism as the heart of Judaism immediately establishes the uniqueness of Judaism. Christianity can hardly approach the standards of religion of reason in which ethics and duty are primary to man's being man. Judaism reflects this clearly in asserting the primacy of law in the religious life. Christianity may have a sense of ethics but this is blunted because its greatest stress is on faith. Judaism's superiority is likewise seen in its idea of God as well, where it is strictly monotheistic. Both God's unity and uniqueness are compromised in Christianity by the doctrine of the Trinity and more specifically by the incarnation. This interpretation is confirmed by the relative position of miracle in Judaism. There it hardly plays a role whereas it is central to Christianity. So Judaism is supremely religion of reason and therefore insofar as a Jew is modern that modernity will commend to him not Christianity but Judaism.

There is an interesting aftereffect of Cohen's position. Most of the leaders of American liberal Judaism were educated in Germany and therefore came under the sway of Cohen's interpretation of Judaism. They heard of their faith as religion of reason and taught it as such to their students and thus to the American Jewish laity. It is therefore common to hear Judaism, particularly in its progressive versions, spoken of as a rational religion. People then expect that Judaism should somehow be susceptible of rational demonstration or explanation. Attempts to speak of Judaism in other terms, say, "mysticism" or "existentialism," cannot be tolerated. They are, by very method, no longer liberal Judaism. Cohen's religion of reason is the unconscious paradigm for modern Jewish theology. However, what Cohen meant by "reason" is hardly what the word denotes today. For Cohen, not only science but ethical will and aesthetic appreciation were equally legitimately part of the realm of reason. That is far broader than most contemporary ways of understanding the term. Were technical philosophy to adopt such a broader vision, it might indeed be possible to speak even now of rational religion. With the term restricted by most thinkers to that which can be empirically verified or falsified, the possibilities for a religion of such reason are few to the point of meaninglessness.

That problem is foreshadowed in the way in which the man he suggested as most likely to carry on his work, Leo Baeck, departed from it. Baeck was a young rabbi at the turn of the century when Cohen's mature philosophic works were appearing in print. Baeck won wide recognition with the appearance of his book *The Essence of Judaism* in 1905. This work had been stimulated by the extraordinary reception given Adolf von Harnack's volume of 1900, *The Essence of Christianity* (entitled in translation *What Is Christianity?*). Baeck's effort has often been seen in terms of a Jewish response to Harnack, and in part it is. Baeck, who always had a strong polemic thrust to his expositions of Judaism, never mentions Harnack, yet the continual comparisons of his Judaism to Harnack's Christianity are obvious. Where the latter is centered around one man and his teaching, Judaism knows no single, dominating figure but rather the continuity of teachers working within the life and history of the Jewish people. Where Christianity early knows a major dislocation of its pristine faith which needs to be reasserted by a Protestant Reformation renewed again now in Protestant liberalism, Judaism knows an essential continuity of teaching expressed in different forms over the ages but remaining essentially true. Where the fundamental message of the church is a love toward man which stems from being loved by God, Judaism knows the more stringent and social ethical relationship to God in which the deed rather than the heart is the central concern. These answering affirmations are critical to Baeck's understanding of Judaism. Yet when the two books are read many decades later, particularly with the figure of Cohen standing nearby for contrast, it is clear that Baeck has learned so much from Harnack, or from the philosopher of history Wilhelm Dilthey who put the approach into abstract terms, that their fundamental methodological stance is nearly identical.

The term "essence" was well known and much abused in nineteenth-century German thought. Hegel is not to be blamed for the arbitrariness of later thinkers trying to show how spirit had made itself manifest in various historical epochs or cultural institutions. The intellectual turning point from such aberration came when men began to study the historical data in great detail to see what would emerge from it. Harnack was the ideal German philological historian whose mastery of the detailed sources of Christian history could not be denied. He brought this approach to a climax by leaving his historical researches momentarily to let the data speak for itself through him. Having immersed himself so thoroughly in the history of Christianity, he was now hopeful its essence would attain utterance in his description of it.

That, too, was what Baeck proposed to do for Judaism. He was not a philosopher and did not begin his work by establishing rational categories with which to explain Judaism. He was more a historian, in that special sense of German, idealist history in which the researcher so identifies with his materials, known in meticulous detail, that he is now able to speak for them. He was not only free of philosophical preconditions but of the theologian's customary insistence on beginning with revelation. The validity of Judaism was not to rest on a unique event at Sinai but rather on the truth of the central ideas which the people had over the ages continually maintained. Baeck maintained that stance toward the interpretation of Judaism through all his writings. Though he disagreed with the Jewish existentialists Rosenzweig and Buber he showed more sympathy for their writings than Harnack did toward Karl Barth, perhaps because the Barthian neo-orthodoxy was so much greater a departure from liberalism than was Jewish existentialism.

In terms of essence there is not much to separate the rabbi-historian Leo Baeck from the philosopher of Judaism, Hermann Cohen, for what Baeck found to be the essence of Judaism was ethical monotheism. That was what Cohen had been saying and what in *Religion of Reason* he would later expound in a more substantial way. It seems hardly likely that Baeck would have highlighted the place of ethics and monotheism in Judaism as he did had it not been for the continuing work of Cohen. That his historical approach established as essential what Cohen's philosophical system-building showed to be rational could only serve to bring the two men closer together.

Baeck, however, departed from Cohen in basing his exposition of Judaism not only on man's sense of the ethical but on his religious consciousness as well. To some extent that may be found in the first edition of *The Essence of Judaism,* but it dominates the greatly expanded and revised second edition. It appeared in 1922, and the seven subsequent editions followed it with only minor alterations. Baeck did not abandon or modify the Neo-Kantian insistence on the primacy of ethics. He wrote: "From the very beginning of the real, the prophetic, religion of Israel, its cardinal factor was the moral law. Judaism is not merely ethical, but *ethics constitutes its principle, its essence* [italics in the original]. Monotheism came into being as a result of the realization of the absolute character of the moral law." So much is still Neo-Kantian. But the added sentence shows the move away, "The moral consciousness teaches about God." The word "consciousness" is highly significant. Set in the context of the rest of the book it refers to a different realm of experience from the one to which philosophy is limited by the Neo-Kantians. Here one hears the overtones of Schleiermacher's interpretation of religion in terms, not even of practical reason, but in terms of man's self-consciousness, particularly that self-consciousness which Schleiermacher identifies as religious consciousness. Baeck takes great pains to make certain his reliance on this sense is not confused with that of Schleiermacher, which is good reason to think he was not oblivious of his debt. Perhaps, too, though he does not mention him or speak explicitly in his categories, Baeck was influenced by Rudolf Otto's well-received book, *The Idea of the Holy*. It appeared in 1917 and by its fine reception gave new vigor to the notion of religion arising from a unique level of consciousness.

Baeck's addition of this new principle of explanation to complement the ethical does not, however, strengthen it, for it shatters the philosophic integrity of the Neo-Kantian argument. What Cohen had done in his carefully integrated system is fully dependent upon the definition of what "pure" knowledge, "pure" will, "pure" feeling are. Once that purity is broken, once what is beyond the Kantian sense of the legitimately rational is admitted as a basis for consideration and judgment, the entire system falls. For Baeck then to argue from a special religious consciousness is tantamount to repudiating the continuing validity, better, the sufficiency, of the Neo-Kantian explanation.

Baeck surely realized what he was doing but he never explained why he took this step. Perhaps he could not admit having made a major methodological departure, for that would constitute a break in the identity of self with the historic material in Dilthey's sense. Or it may simply have been the maturing of what was always part of his understanding but one which he had never yet properly expressed. He was probably not concerned with the decline of professional interest in Neo-Kantianism which took place around World War I. The most reasonable explanation seems to be that he was a rabbi in concern as in profession, and his primary interest was in the quality of the religious life produced by a philosophy of Judaism. The Neo-Kantian exposition had established the centrality of God to man's life but did so in terms of God as an idea, a concept, and it made ethics, which are necessarily universal, not Jewish practice, man's fundamental duty. Such a God is too abstract to elicit piety and hardly provides a reason for expanding ethics into religious observance. That judgment is not really fair to the Cohenian position. For an "idea" list, there is no reality greater than that of a systematically required rational idea, and certainly there is no more fundamental or integrative idea than that of God. Moreover, Cohen and his followers had exposed the ethics implicit in every area of Jewish practice. (Had Cohen done nothing else but spur this ethical hermeneutic which opened up the most diverse areas of Jewish life to show their modern value, his achievement would have been great.) Nonetheless, to the devout, there remains an unbearable distance between what philosophy says religion ought to be and what religion knows as its reality. Whether in response to the special yearning which arose among men after World War I, or whether it was simply the reassertion of traditional Jewish piety, Baeck now introduced the felt, subjective level of religion into his explanation of Judaism.

The problem is already to be seen in Cohen's own wrestling with the proper place of religion in his system. In his early works he would not give it an autonomous place in the rational activities of the human spirit. It was not the equal of knowledge, ethics, and aesthetics. By 1915 he had reconsidered his previous complete subordination of religion to ethics and now argued, not for a realm of religious truth outside of reason and detached from the ethical, but for its special character, its unique identity in man's life. Where ethics deals with mankind in general, religion concentrates on the individual. Where ethics is concerned with doing, religion can equally comprehend the realm of the undone or done badly, sin, repentance, atonement. One almost hears Kierkegaard's stages here. Now, however, the two schools interpreting Cohen divide. The existentialists, under Rosenzweig's leadership, argue that Cohen's growing appreciation of Judaism had burst the old Neo-Kantian boundaries and that he was on the verge of stating an independent religious position as is manifest in his posthumous volume. His more rationalistically minded followers, however, seek to find ways to maintain the integrity of his philosophic enterprise, and insist that though religion has gained status, it never rises to the level where it can supply a truth independent of or more comprehensive than that given by ethics. This is probably what lies behind the difference in the title of the two editions of his posthumous volume. The first one begins with the article *die, Die Religion der Vernunft,* almost as if in Judaism one finds in quite particularistic form the religion of reason itself. The second edition is titled simply *Religion der Vernunft,* . . . the universal, rational phenomenon which one may indeed find in Jewish sources but obviously is not to be too closely linked with them or any other historical concretization.

Whatever scholarship may yet find to have been Cohen's path, Baeck knew that the living experience of religion as piety had to be given equal status with it as ethics. That would restore the personal tone to religion which the Neo-Kantian interpretation had tended to restrict to the mental. Baeck was not able to join the existentialists in their risk-filled explorations. He remained too much indebted to Cohen for that, but he passed beyond him nonetheless in utilizing Schleiermacher's category of religious self-consciousness. It should not be surprising, therefore, that paradox and dialectic are major motifs in Baeck's thinking. He is constantly shuttling between positions that are in tension with one another. The interplay of exposition in terms of ethics or the religious consciousness is fundamental, though not all of Baeck's polarities stem from this basic dichotomy of approach.

Characteristically, Baeck grounds the ethical in the mystery which the religious consciousness senses behind the creation. Both Kant and Cohen knew the philosophic desirability of extending ethics beyond themselves, rationally self-sustaining for them though they be. In Kant they lead on to the practical knowledge that there is a God who guarantees their fulfillment. In Cohen the idea of God guarantees that the infinite moral task will have infinite reality in which to work itself out. Those philosophic assertions are thin and pale compared to the religious man's certainty that the commandments come to him personally, that they are an address from what is most real in the universe, that his failure to do them properly fills him with dread, that there will come a day in which righteousness will be triumphant on earth and visible to all. Religious experience testifies to what lies beyond the ethical, to the God who has the right to issue imperatives and make them so categorical. Reason cannot reach such a realm but it is a very present consciousness to the man of faith. For Baeck, ethics without this mysterious grounding in God is mere moralism. For Judaism, there can be no ethics which does not stem from God and relate man directly to him. To deny that connection is to begin to sunder one's spiritual connection with Judaism and that is the great danger of the contemporary culture. With the rejection of God the rejection of ethics cannot be long delayed. That has been the gloomy truth of modern history.

However, it will not do to glorify man's religious feelings to the point where they have full sway. That might lead to an a-ethical religion of self-concern or utter inwardness. Even directed outward such emotions might produce fanaticism or superstition. Having suffered from these states over the years, Judaism cannot base itself on unbridled feeling. Rather, its religious consciousness may take form only through the ethical. Should it threaten to emerge in any other guise, it must be rejected as temptation. However, when it issues forth in the ethical realm, it brings power and strength to the ethical, receiving in turn the secure guidance it needs if man is to be man and God is properly to be served. Here, Baeck decisively and by name dissociates himself from Schleiermacher and his sense of religion as absolute dependence. That Baeck finds intolerable because it renders man ethically inert and so destroys his dignity. Practically, too, by Baeck's time German Romanticism had made clear its great potential for viciousness and barbarism, not the least by its close link with a growing anti-Semitism. Schleiermacher would have despised such an extension of his thought, but one thinking about these matters decades later could not fail to be concerned. Baeck's debt to Cohen and the Kantian stream in German Jewish thought is nowhere seen more clearly than in his insistence on containing the religious experience within the structure of ethical command, though it itself is based ultimately on a romantic not a rational foundation.

Baeck's exposition of Judaism is typically liberal, saying very much more about man, his ethical sense and his consciousness of the Divine, than it says about God, who he is and what, if anything, he does—but that man is now spoken of in terms of his full self-consciousness. So Baeck argues against the philosophers that the idea of God has little more religious value than any other pure idea. Even the theoretical question of God's existence is not important, but only whether the individual feels his life bound up with eternity and from that receives an inner consciousness of humility, of courage, of peace. Man's certainty that God is real comes not from some rational demonstration that he is the First Cause or the one who orders nature. He finds it rather in what has happened to his life, the inner consistency that it now has gained, the moral power that has been added to it, the sense of answer to his deepest longings and questions, the knowledge that all of life must be lived in response to a question being put to him from what is beyond him. Is, then, God himself personal? Of that, Baeck insists, nothing can be said and nothing was said in Judaism. God is not to be understood as a God of qualities or one about whom dogmas may be stated. Judaism knows no dogmas. However, since man's consciousness of God is as one close and responsive, one who legitimately penetrates into the innermost existence of man, "He is therefore understood personally and regarded as personal. In the depths of man there lives and grows the personal." This is typical of Baeck's use of religious consciousness to reclaim traditionally Jewish aspects of the Divine which were inaccessible to the Neo-Kantians.

Yet Baeck immediately balances this emphasis on personalism with ethical rigor. The danger of such intimate talk about God is an anthropomorphism that comes to be taken seriously by believers, destroying the transcendence of God and thereby vitiating the authority of the ethical. The rabbis and the medieval philosophers in particular waged a protracted battle to overcome this error. They succeeded but only at the price of turning God into an abstraction which might become a denial of the innermost reality of man's experience. That danger is finally overcome in Judaism by asserting a fundamental paradox about God, that the exalted, transcendent God is nonetheless the present, personal God. Nothing may stand between man and his God, but that God must remain the God of the infinite heights and depths of creation. The ethical and devotional realm are simultaneously maintained.

The sensitivity with which Baeck uses his two interpretive devices is well illustrated in his treatment of the Biblical conception of God's wrath or jealous nature. These terms cannot be rejected simply on the grounds that they are anthropomorphisms, for then one would have to reject such meaningful symbolic expressions for God as "Father." The problem is, rather, meaning. What is being given human voice in these strange terms? It is man's sense of the exclusiveness of the ethical. Genuine morality always implies a protest and resistance to immorality. It is in its very essence exclusive, categorical about its imperatives. It will not have any intercourse with evil. It sees in any trace of unrighteousness a denial of God and a perversion of man's calling. To become involved with moral wrong is to enter a realm without meaning, without value, without reality. It is to leave life and choose death. Evil is not to be compromised with or tolerated. God's jealousy is the powerful way man describes this fundamental reality and thus gives form to the sense that God, the source of the ethical command, is one and only one.

What might have seemed the most unethical of terms for God is now seen as highly ethical. Again and again Baeck does just that with traditional Judaism, giving it new and unexpected moral power. He is continually citing the classics of Judaism, the Bible, the prayer book, the rabbis, and making many an often quoted phrase refract a new light. Yet whenever he carries out such an ethical transvaluation, it is precisely man's inner apprehension of the ethical situation extended to its religious depth that shapes the fullness of his Judaism. The ethical content of Jewish belief may turn up in unfamiliar places and in new ways in the expected ones, but always there is a simultaneous discovery of man, of who the reader is and what he should be becoming.

Rather than sketch out the rest of Baeck's universal doctrine, it will be more useful in estimating his continuing validity to examine his theology of the people of Israel, its mission and its law. There is an additional advantage to this procedure. It will clarify the integrity of his thinking as it developed. Baeck was not primarily concerned with these themes in his early book. There he was discussing the essence of Judaism and that, by philosophical necessity, had to be universal. So it is only in the final few pages that Baeck treats of particularistic doctrines in some detail. That is not to say that he was not concerned with them or did not think them important in Judaism. The burden of that book was simply to establish Israel's universal message. Having done that, he had provided the context in which alone such a rationale could be given meaningful form.

Baeck's priority in theological problems underwent a shift in the twenties, undoubtedly under the impact of the revolution in Protestant theology and the alarming growth of Nazism. In 1932 he published an essay "Theology and History" in which he states the need for a theology of Judaism in its particularity. He warns against importing Christian terminology and methods into Judaism, for these will undoubtedly distort any description of Judaism. That is coupled with a plea for continued use of the science of Judaism with its critical approach to the Jewish past only now carried on for the purpose of clarifying the continuing validity of Judaism. He seems to be arguing against importing the Biblicism of Barth or the existentialism of Bultmann or Tillich into Judaism. Baeck insists that the historic continuity of Judaism, seen in its essence, is the one firm basis for Jewish theology. What changed for Baeck was not the method of doing theology, which still follows Dilthey, but only the focus of concern. Here, too, he stands with Harnack who opposed the Barthian theology strongly, and a comparison of the two men in this period would be of great scholarly interest.

Baeck finally fulfilled his own proposal in the work he published after World War II called, to translate literally, *This People: Jewish Existence.* The circumstances of its appearance reveal a triumph of the human spirit which alone would make the book memorable. When Hitler came to power, Baeck was the leading liberal rabbi of Berlin and such a significant figure in the German Jewish community that he was then named president of its representative organization. The dignity that he brought to a justly proud community about to undergo a tragedy unlike anything perpetrated upon men by civilized men—and how can one compare this to what uncivilized man did in his barbarity?—has been described most movingly by survivors of that period. Despite many opportunities to leave the country, including several official trips abroad, he stayed with his people and was eventually sent to a concentration camp. His demeanor there, the way he endured his sufferings, his unflagging concern for others, the efforts he made to keep them human by teaching them, from memory, the great humanistic classics, his refusal to be less than ethical or to let the Nazis make him less than human, made him one of the heroic figures of an impossible situation. By error, chance, the sacrifice of others, by his spirit and the grace of Providence, the seventy-year-old rabbi survived Theresienstadt. He went to London and brought with him the scraps of paper on which were written the book that he had started before his internment and continued work on in the camp. That was the birth of Part One of *Dieses Volk: Jüdische Existenz.* Part Two was the product of his remaining years.

The title of the book bespeaks the new concern. Where once he wrote about Judaism, here he is concerned with the Jewish people. Then he was concerned with essence. Now it is existence which matters. Yet Baeck had not given up his universally oriented ethical approach for an existentialist, particularist approach to Judaism. *This People Israel* turns out to be an extension of what he had written in *The Essence of Judaism* a quarter of a century before. The savage immorality of Germans, the pious indifference of the rest of the world, the new loneliness of an emancipated Jewry, the glory of the State of Israel aborning, did not make him feel that his fundamental position required revision. What he did was give it more ample statement and apply it to the history of the Jewish people.

Neither Baeck's God nor his universalist emphasis lend themselves to the traditional Jewish doctrine of chosenness. God may be associated with man's sense of mysterious depth to his createdness, but Baeck does not find this a basis for saying God acts in history. Rather, since his relationship with man always takes on a universal ethical structure, any notion of chosenness in which there is a sense of radical particularity is necessarily precluded. The God of ethical monotheism must by his very nature be equally available to all men—a concept known to traditional Judaism—and not be available to any of them in any unique way—a negation of the paradoxical, complementary Jewish faith.

All men can know God and some men everywhere do. This universally possible understanding came to the Hebrews as it might to any people. Only, in their case, the understanding became decisive for what they were to be as a people. They applied to their people what they knew to be true for all human existence—that their community must live up to the demands of ethical monotheism. They shaped their folk character, they staked all their future on this fundamental religious insight. Remaining faithful to that vision despite periods of infidelity, they became conscious of themselves as different from the rest of the peoples. They realized that they had become uniquely pledged to God. They and the idea of ethical monotheism had become one. What had been an intuition now became a mission for the future of ethical monotheism in history, and was now linked with them. They were the hope of humanity if it was ever truly to be human. So they lived in history not only for their own sake but for all men. In this knowledge they found the strength to survive the terrors they underwent, for they knew that if they succumbed, so did hope for man.

All human communities could and should do that but in actual fact they do not. It is not in the availability of the idea that religious particularity can be asserted but only in the historic actuality of its appropriation and continuing expression.

The Jews are chosen only in the sense that when they are

confronted with God's command to be human as all people are, they choose to respond to it as a people. When through the years this becomes their deepest consciousness of themselves, they call themselves a chosen people, the people of the Covenant. Once again Baeck's two principles balance out. What ethical theory had made improbable the coordinate theory of religious consciousness has now explained. The content remains universal; the way of thinking about oneself, based on history, establishes the particularity.

This position has existential rather than mere historical validity only if it can be argued that no other community carries the same understanding through history. In *The Essence of Judaism,* Baeck had distinguished world religions as of two basic types, world-affirming and world-rejecting. He considers Judaism the classic example of the former type and he calls it a religion of ethical optimism. He does not deny that there are ethical teachings in religions of the other sort, of which Buddhism is the prototype, only their essential stance toward the world is withdrawal. Such ethics gains its objectives by not investing too much in expectations and therefore is not contentious. It loses that gain, however, by not being able to care deeply even about righteousness or to be outraged by immorality. His more extensive polemic, once that distinction is made, is carried out against Christianity which would seem to share Judaism's basic faith about God and the centrality of ethics. Baeck does not see Christianity as an equal to Judaism because he finds Christian self-consciousness differing radically from that of Judaism. His ideas are developed extensively in an essay called "Romantic Religion," published first in 1922 and later given somewhat expanded form. Baeck also uses the typological method here and identifies two types of religious experience. The one, the classic, is positive, activist, outgoing, social, ethical, deed oriented, rational, masculine. The other, the romantic, is passive in the face of reality, individualistic, self-centered, inward, concerned with faith and its content, confirming itself in feelings, emphasizing grace. It has a feminine cast. Such pure types exist only in thought but history knows religions which are outstanding representatives of these possibilities. Judaism is closest to the classic type while Christianity is the finest example of romantic religion. Baeck ranges through the breadth of the Christian experience, Catholic as well as Protestant, to exhibit what, from the standpoint of religion of reason, are its most undesirable features. He draws on the complete arsenal of arguments forged by the Jewish polemicists of the preceding century, particularly his Neo-Kantian forebears. Baeck continually contrasts the ethical monotheism of Judaism with the grace mysticism of Christianity, to the obvious discredit of the latter. To argue that Judaism is not the single community bearing ethical monotheism through history is to fail to understand the fundamental nature of Christianity.

Subjectivity is the problem of all typologies, and Baeck's departure to a private realm of judgment is the dominant fact of this essay. Why there are just two types, why these are romantic and classic, why Judaism and Christianity are the chief representatives, how one would deal with all the countervailing evidence in both religions, is only asserted. It is never argued, probably because it cannot be. Baeck does admit that Judaism has romantic elements and Christianity classical ones, but he does not investigate this to see how far it goes. He seems, rather, to be throwing it out as a methodological sop to take care of the obvious traits in both religions which go against his types. Baeck speaks of Judaism in liberalistic terms as an ethical and rational faith. He does not contrast this with a similar interpretation of Christianity but with a rather more traditional Protestantism or Catholicism. Either he should have argued the virtue of his Judaism against that of, say, Harnack's or he should have used a nonliberal view of the essence of Judaism to set alongside what he here deals with as Christianity. Only that would be fair, but Baeck could not see the problem. He was so fully committed to his method that he could not believe that what he had said was the essence of Judaism was not objectively visible, but a highly subjective reading. What he and Harnack, in the self-assurance of their humanistic, scientific approach to the interpretation of history, took as self-evident now appears as self-satisfaction masquerading as science. There is a Jewish self-respect which rises to moments of grandeur in Baeck's treatment of the relations between Judaism and Christianity. Yet Baeck does not wish to be treated here as the advocate but as the scholar. In that respect the essay does not stand the test of time. As it falls it carries with it Baeck's entire argument for Jewish uniqueness and continuity.

There is another major implication of Baeck's thesis that the content of Judaism is fully universal, though held uniquely by the Jews. All mankind ought to possess this faith, and by virtue of having it, Israel recognizes its responsibility to share its faith with mankind. Baeck interprets quite actively the idea that the Jews have a mission to mankind. Exemplification is not enough for him. A campaign of proselytization is needed. Though Jews in medieval times did not seek converts and seemed rather to discourage them, it appears that this was largely the result of external pressures. While the rabbis do occasionally protest against proselytes, the overwhelming majority of their statements are positive. When the Jews were free, they proselytized, and today in all dignity and faithfulness to their belief they should do so again.

That responsibility to make ethical monotheism the living faith of mankind is not only a mission but a mandate. The idea has made its way into history through this particular people. It cannot now be detached from Israel, for significant spiritual ideas do not become reality among men without being borne by specific peoples or cultures. Others may now come to know the meaning of ethical monotheism but they are not responsible for its fate in history. Israel must persevere not just for its own sake but for all mankind.

The achievement of such an ethical perspective is no easy task for most men. They quickly relapse to paganism. Hence, Israel's task is not short-term. Endurance is critical and stubbornness an ethical imperative. With Israel God's representative people, for a Jew to exist is already a commandment. That realism must be coupled with Baeck's Jewish optimism. Man's history and Israel's service are not in vain. Man can achieve a time in which the commandment addressed to him is fulfilled. That is the faith which has enabled Israel to survive these many centuries. So Israel now stands in history not only as a witness to its truth but to the efficacy of hope. A despairing mankind needs Israel to remind it that man need not be overcome. Baeck devotes the bulk of *This People Israel* to showing how the different stages of Jewish history made their own unique contribution to this continuing Jewish service, enriching but not distorting it.

To carry on through history as well as to bring its faith to life, the people of Israel created Jewish law. The distinction between commandment and law is critical. Baeck is quite consistent in his separation of the categories but rarely makes explicit the difference between what would usually be considered almost identical terms. "Commandment" is a term properly used only for that which comes from God himself, to Baeck the ethical in its broad understanding. Coming from God it is fundamental and, in effect, unchanging. Man may come to know it better or express it more fully but it is not subject to his will or imagination. One finds the ethical commandment implicit in almost everything in Jewish law. That is what establishes its most immediate claim upon Jews. By doing Jewish law, they fulfill their fundamental human responsibility. Yet there is an obvious distance between modern ethics and Jewish law. That has become particularly visible with the radical change of the Jewish social situation, for now many of the old prescriptions no longer have the same ethical effect. With ethics as essence and thus entitled to priority, Baeck is a liberal who favors change in the law to allow commandment to become more evident in law. Yet he does not advocate dispensing with Jewish law altogether because law, though it must be attuned to commandment, goes beyond it and is responsive to a second imperative. It serves not only God but the Jewish people in pursuit of its mission. The law is the instrument of Jewish cohesion and survival in history. It unites the people, though it may be quite widely dispersed or over the ages find itself in new climates, economies, or political orders. If it did only that, it would have no compelling power. However, its high ethical content not only keeps Israel alive as a people but loyal to its task, and it protects the folk against the attacks of its enemies. The law separates it from mankind so the Jews have a distance from their barbarities, and it enjoins an inner life of warmth and beauty which is the most effective antidote to men's vicious devisings.

Even this sketch of Baeck's thought shows, it is to be hoped, that it is an imposing intellectual and religious achievement. It is, thus far, the last of the great Jewish universalist structures. For if the requirements of a modern Jewish theology are that it be both modern and yet authentically Jewish, it and with it the entire Neo-Kantian approach fail contemporary scrutiny on both grounds. To say a word about the Jewish inadequacy first will be easier, since, as interpreted here, that seems to have been Baeck's own motive for moving beyond Cohen.

It was suggested that Baeck introduced religious consciousness into his theology to make possible a personal relationship to God. The question Baeck seemed to be answering was why one needed religion at all if one knew and lived by philosophy. He could not answer that question by philosophical means, for that would already give away the case. Baeck therefore established the autonomy of religion by insisting upon the validity of the religious consciousness yet he kept it from the excesses of Romanticism by linking it firmly to the ethical.

The more fundamental problem created by philosophy, approaching Judaism through a framework of universal truth, had, however, not been overcome. Baeck may have gone beyond Neo-Kantianism but he remained in the world of philosophical idealism. As long as the essential content of Judaism is universal and can be known on that level, a series of almost unanswerable questions arise. If ethical monotheism is the essence of Judaism, then why does one need Judaism now that this universal truth is reasonably clear? Why chance distorting the message by particularizing it? Why take the risks of being Jewish when even a good philosophy will teach ethical monotheism? Is there not even an ethical responsibility to succeeding generations to spare them the possible suffering entailed in perpetuating the Jewish people when the teaching they have carried can now be given in a direct intellectual form? Since Baeck has made the people of Israel only an instrumental value serving a higher universal truth, he has made it possible to argue that one should choose a less dangerous instrument which might accomplish the same end. Baeck's only intellectual response to this argument seems alien to his system, though it possesses two explanatory principles. A Hegelian could consistently argue that an idea requires a people to carry it through history, but such an assertion has no relation either to the ethical or the religious experience of man. Without some new elaboration of the way in which the mysterious ground of creation makes itself manifest, this idea has no place in the Baeckian system or else is asserted as dogma, an equally unthinkable possibility.

The stance becomes untenable when the questions are raised about Jewish practice. Assuming the Jewish people is the bearer of ethical monotheism in history, why need a Jew do more than the good and believe in God? Is not all the rest of Jewish practice secondary? If one is faithful to ethics and loyal to the Jews, why must he get involved with a lunar calendar, Semitic celebrations, and Hebraic liturgy? Although they might enrich his life and solidify the people, they are also a special burden in a society in which the range of activities reinforcing ethics is great and many seem more consistent with ethical universalism, since they are not conducive to parochialism but to overcoming the divisions between groups. On a practical level that objection to Jewish observance turns up in the continual question, Isn't one a good Jew if he is ethical and believes in God in his heart? In a day when there is so much to do most people are quite satisfied if they can manage to live the life of essence. The helping instrumentalities, particularly when they mean special effort and special burdens, they are quite content to let fall away. That tells much of the story of what liberal Judaism has meant and has not meant to American Jewry. For a generation which was so solidly Jewish that it could make universalizing its major concern without losing its Jewishness, Baeck's system was compelling. In the contemporary world, where Jews are substantially integrated into the general culture and the continuing question is what can their Jewishness mean to them, Baeck's position fails to explicate a fully authentic pattern of Jewish existence.

That failing is so obvious to anyone who has tried to work in the contemporary Jewish community that little needs to be said about Baeck's intellectual appeal. He spoke with the certainty of the Neo-Kantian tradition about the moral law and he rises to creative heights in expounding its place in Judaism. Yet that understanding of the moral experience as reliable, rational, and self-authenticating is absent in current philosophy and contradicted by modern culture. As history has posed its tests or personal existence has plunged men into crisis, they have discovered that ambiguity and uncertainty, not clarity and categorical imperatives, were placed before them. Men still want to be moral but in the torturous situations in which they often find themselves they do not hear the ethical command sound with the certainty Baeck assumed it had. Their religious consciousness has not eased their difficulties. They have felt and acted on the most demonic passions, hoping that emotions would provide a certainty which conscience no longer could. In Baeck's trials he remained firm. Modern men would like to emulate his character but they do not see how what he said would lead them there. He seems the last great exemplar of a tradition rather than the enunciator of a new style for a new age.

Besides, Baeck never clarifies how the religious consciousness and ethical understanding are bound together. Why does inner experience need to be limited in action to what the ethical can allow? Why must the ethical command rest on a mysterious ground? Philosophically these limits go against the teachings of the intellectual schools which validated the two principles. If it is argued that this is rather what Judaism sees as the higher unity, then one must finally turn again to the ultimate question and ask just how Baeck knows this. What is the methodology by which he ascertains the essence of Judaism? What are the criteria by which he knows what is unessential and secondary? Surely his proposal, persuasive as it is, is not the self-understanding of the Jewish tradition. Following Dilthey's theory of interpretation based on self-identification with the historical sources here seems to say more about self than about the character of the tradition. More important, the interpreter is not aware of his subjectivity and thus less able to guard himself and his reader against its excesses. A modern reader wants to know what is meant by the essence of a tradition and how it is determined. Then one will want to examine the representativeness of the data that demonstrates it to be so and particularly the treatment of apparently contradictory material. All this is hidden in Baeck in a way that makes him appear almost authoritarian to the rigorous skepticism of the contemporary inquirer.

Yet there is a lasting greatness to Baeck, indeed to the entire Neo-Kantian tradition in Judaism, which remains central to the thought of any liberal Judaism. Not only is man and his autonomous creativity placed firmly toward the center of Jewish theology, at the least as God's partner, but his ethical activity is given a priority that nothing in his religious life can usurp. One cannot any longer read the prophets without a burning sensitivity to the proper hierarchy of religious action. Ritual, prayer, study—all may be vital to the ongoing religious life. They cannot substitute for the way man acts toward man. It remains the perennial temptation of any institution to place its needs above human misery. It is a special temptation of a minority and oppressed people to be so concerned for its preservation that it neglects broad, humanitarian values to attend to survival. A folk newly released from the ghetto naturally finds it difficult to associate its sense of commandment with the needs of all mankind. Yet anyone who has been sensitized by Cohen, Baeck, and their followers to the fundamental ethical quality of the Jewish tradition should not lose his way. Without a universalistic moral intensity, Judaism can no longer be true to itself.

Moreover, these men showed that it was possible to give a full-scale statement of Judaism in modern terms. Indeed, in Cohen it raised the possibility that Judaism might satisfactorily be expressed in philosophic terms. Such a fusion of Judaism and philosophy seems most unlikely today, and that older synthesis no longer seems adequate. The problem has become only more complex, for Baeck clarified the point that any adequate treatment of Judaism must be as true to the religious spirit as it is to the inquiring mind. The idea of God cannot supplant and does not make possible the love of God. And both must be confirmed in a validation of the people of Israel's continued existence and its distinctive way of life. The fundamental questions had been asked in a properly sophisticated way and some answers of continuing validity had been given. No wonder all subsequent Jewish religious thought builds on this foundation!

5

MORDECAI KAPLAN: THE LIMITS OF NATURALISM

If philosophy is the child of leisure, 1934 would seem a strange year for the appearance of the first major American philosophy of Judaism. The time was one of crisis both for America and for Judaism. The economic depression was at its depths and with it came a lack of morale, a rise of hostility, and a pervading anger born of frustration. Every stress was felt with special force in the American Jewish community. Jewishness had always been, at least, a matter of difference. In those gloomy depression days it had become a handicap, to many, a catastrophe. Nor could they easily forget it. Anti-Semitism was an open, publicly approved, well-supported movement.

Much of the mood of American Jewry was flight—from the Jewishness that was connected with remaining an alien to the humanitarian virtues of democracy which rewarded talent impartially.

Into this disheartening scene there came a message of Jewish hope. With the publication of his by now classic work *Judaism as a Civilization,* Mordecai Kaplan emerged as the intellectual focus of the generation. Not that he had been unknown before the book appeared. For many years he had taught at the Jewish Theological Seminary of America, influencing scores of men going into the burgeoning Conservative rabbinate and all areas of Jewish education. At the same time he had been influential with Jewish social workers through his efforts to transform the settlement house into what has become the Jewish Center. Now, as a mature thinker, he challenged American Jewry with a full-scale analysis of its situation.

Ever since, the sense of crisis in Jewish life has rarely been absent in Mordecai Kaplan's writings. His perennial premise is that once the Jew knows who he is in contemporary society, his doubts and insecurities will vanish and his energies will find proper Jewish and human expression. So his goal in all his writings has been to articulate a social philosophy of the Jews.

The special Jewish difficulties, as Kaplan sees them, are a reflection of the upheaval that has affected all the peoples and religions of the Western world in modern times. Two terms may be used to epitomize it: nationalism and naturalism. Both are used quite broadly.

Nationalism means not just the nineteenth-century ideal by which ethnic groups sought political self-expression, that is, to become a state. It must encompass that entire process by which monarchy gave way to democracy and the conception of society as divinely, hence statically, ordered gave way to the secular state. It was founded on social contract and in it, therefore, all men had equal rights. For the Jew, nationalism meant emancipation, the end of ghetto existence both physically and spiritually. Becoming a full participant in the life of his country was on every level a radical change for him.

The modernity of the secular state is synonymous with naturalism, which is precisely the rejection of supernaturalism. Man now begins with and limits his thought to this world and the natural order of existence. Naturalism sees in the scientific approach to reality, including man and society, the most reliable method of ascertaining truth concerning all matters of human interest. It focuses on man and his welfare, rather than God and his will, as the purpose of reasonable human striving. It is a shift from theocentrism to humanism, and

Kaplan often uses the term "humanism" in this man-centered but not God-denying sense.

What such a methodological humanism does to the old religious emphases on supernatural revelation, miracles, and otherworldly salvation, is revolutionary. Not just God's word, but God himself, must be found in, not above, the natural order; miracles are dismissed as unscientific; and this world, the only one man can know, is where he must seek salvation.

Most modern men in fact live by these views, though some are unconscious of it. Kaplan never tires of berating those who still use the old religious slogans when it is clear from their evasions and sometimes from their direct statements that they no longer hold a traditional faith. If there is to be a truly contemporary understanding of reality, it must be coherent with the philosophy implicit in modern science, and if there is to be any reconstruction of the social order, it must be based on the scientific study of man's social development. That means using the studies of human society as well as the research on the history of religion to discover what religion truly is and how it functions. Sociology thus becomes the critical science for Kaplan's naturalistic view of Judaism. He explicitly refers to Durkheim, from whom much of his social orientation is taken, when he affirms that for modern man religion is given its function and character by scientific observation.

Religion can, however, prove a significant supplement to nationalism and naturalism. Where the state has failed to serve persons but has demanded rather that they serve its needs, religion can rise in prophetic judgment over such moral treachery. The individual is the goal and measure of the social order, not the tool of its increased efficiency. The state may have other purposes than the good of its several citizens. Religion knows man's self-realization is its central goal and cannot be diverted from it as easily as can the state. Within its own institutions and by its social criticism religion can keep alive the pursuit of individual fulfillment. The mystical element of religion is another important adjunct to the naturalistic method. When it means awareness of the mystery of existence and the reality of spiritual values, when it is the sure sense that the universe supports man's strivings, it is indispensable to personal and social progress.

Kaplan's ultimate faith would seem to be in the adequacy of human reason, and by derivation therefrom in man and society. As he pointedly remarks, his view is not that man has fallen, but that he has risen. Yet it must be noted that the resolution is not altogether clear. Ultimately, intuition makes the reason that affirms God and morality superior to the reason that rejects him and human freedom. Why one should follow it rather than the reason which is more strictly naturalistic in its method and antireligious in content remains unclear. For all his emphasis on modern rationality, Kaplan has an old reliance on faith that brings him to his new content.

What do men learn about the nature of religion and its relation to the peoples who uphold them when they are studied from a naturalistic perspective?

An open examiner cannot help being impressed by the absolute universality of religion in human society. Primitive or high, animistic, polytheistic, or agnostic, religion is found wherever there are records of human existence. Modern man need not look for a god who imposes himself upon mankind or believe that the clever manipulations of priests or capitalists engender religion. Its base is man and his needs.

This drive in man can be more clearly identified. It is his urge to self-fulfillment, to utilize his capacities fully. Man's life is a constant search for self-realization and self-expression. That should not be taken to mean that life itself is the highest good. There are ideals without which life itself is not worth living. The accomplishment of this basic human striving, Kaplan regularly calls "salvation." In a naturalistic, this-worldly era, the term obviously cannot have reference to heaven or paradise. Salvation now must be demythologized to mean fulfillment in this world. Religion is the human institution that helps man find it, and as man's need for such consummation is universal, so is his need for religion.

Though religion is social and man is individual, the two are inseparably joined, for salvation cannot be individual alone, but must be communal as well. How can an individual be morally self-fulfilled as long as he lives in a wretched and miserable world? So too no society can claim to have reached its goal as long as its individual members are frustrated and unhappy.

Much of the present-day confusion over religions arises here. Modern man will sometimes admit that aspects of his life are as socially determined as they are personal. Yet when it comes to religion, he often insists that this is a strictly private concern. This, to Kaplan, represents a complete rejection of what modern social science has disclosed about human religiosity. Since the relation of people to religion becomes the "Copernican turning point" in Kaplan's view of Judaism, it is essential that this point be understood.

A people is necessarily prior to its religion. Belonging—to a people—comes before believing—in a creed. One first shares a people's common social existence and consequently shares in their religious life. The individual does not create religion. Rather, his personal needs and desires are given shape and expression by his culture.

What fundamentally differentiates religions, then, is not so much their theological content as their social expression. There can be but one God and one ethics. The truths of religion are as universal as the operation of human reason. They rest upon the common human nature of all mankind. True, some people have not yet attained the level of ethical religion. There are spiritually underdeveloped areas at home as well as abroad. Yet it is clear what mature religion would be.

To this universal content each people brings its own unique system of symbolic expression. Through the years it has come to regard with devotion certain men, events, places, books, acts. These are its sancta, its channels of reverence, and through them a people expresses in its own personal way those religious feelings which are common to all men. Religions ought to differ from one another on the level of sancta, for articulation is necessary for religious sentiment and this must have a particular cultural form. The underlying concepts, on the other hand, are as common to mankind as is the human nature on which religion is ultimately based.

This passionate emphasis on the importance of one's social group to one's individuality pervades all of Kaplan's thinking. He has a great commitment to the continued significance of separate peoples. This goes so far that for him the death of a particular human civilization is almost worse than the death of an individual. That is because a civilization can survive many individuals and generations. While it is conceivable to Kaplan that religions might become fully universal in theology and ethics, it is not conceivable to him that this would mean the end of separate peoples. They are a permanent and enduring feature of human existence.

Following the great early sociologist Sumner, to whom he acknowledges his debt, Kaplan identifies Judaism as the total civilization of the Jewish people. It is thus the organic unity of the people and its relation to its land, its language and literature, its mores, laws, and folkways, its folk sanctions, its arts, and the social structure in which this living entity is expressed and practiced. The great error of the previous liberal thinkers was to identify Judaism as a mere "religion." Kaplan's broader perspective is the foundation of his theory of Jewish life, which he called (based on the model of the pragmatists of the thirties) Jewish Reconstructionism. The implications of this view become clearer when one considers its component aspects.

A land is obviously critical to any people wishing to develop a civilization. The Jews are no exception. The Torah speaks continually of the importance of the Land of Israel to the people and its special obligations because of the Land. Perhaps an otherworldly religion might be able to dispense with its tie to a specific country. Judaism, as a civilization, cannot. Rather, this social point of view makes Kaplan a strong Zionist. A civilization as contrasted to a religion requires one place where it can be fully lived and fully expressed, an indigenous home of its own. But that center having been created, Jews elsewhere may benefit from its cultural creativity and share its civilization. The establishment of a center of authentic folk civilization on the Land of Israel will make it possible for Jews everywhere to perpetuate and fructify their Jewishness wherever they may be. With a land goes a language. Hebrew never died, and, of all the modern national movements which have sought to revive their ancient tongue, Hebrew alone has been truly revitalized. It is indispensable to worldwide Jewish civilization.

The arts, too, now have a place in Judaism. Religious interpretations of Judaism have been puzzled by Jewish folk songs and dances. Secular interpretations have been embarrassed by the largely ritual concern of Jewish art and poetry. All groups should be shocked at the lack of contemporary Jewish artistic expression, or its limit to a few areas.

Social habits are the content of a civilization. They are social in the sense that one acquires them as a member of one's group and not out of purely personal desire. Jewish life has been rich with such folkways ranging from ethical customs to honored recipes. In premodern days most folkways were authorized as religious rites. Modern man cannot understand the term *mitzvot* as "commandments given by God." For him, that can only be a metaphor for the fact that these acts arouse the religious mood in men. They are more likely to be done when seen as folkways. When the commandments are viewed this way they can be changed if they need to be and the creation of new ones is encouraged.

The essence of Jewish group living must, however, always

be its high ethical standards. Without these the individual loses his humanity and any group its rationale. The glory of Judaism has been its long, exemplary ethical concern and practice, personal and communal as well. Nothing less will do today. That is why religion is so central a part of civilization. It authorizes and validates the ethical concern.

This style of living should then be expressed in a pattern of community organization. That, in turn, would strengthen and encourage this conception of Jewish life. There should be an American version of the European Jewish community structure, the *kehillah,* not here an autonomous or governmentally supported body, but a voluntary association of all Jews and Jewish institutions into what Kaplan terms an "organic community." All Jews should have their basic loyalty to the community, organized as such, and the community, in turn, should see to it that the diverse needs of the Jews are met. Thus, to give the most striking example, congregations would be maintained by the community for the groups desiring them and rabbis would be retained by the community as a whole to serve the various communal needs. Such a structure could make possible a new sense of community standards and values. At a mature level of development it could become the basis for democratically articulating new criteria for Jewish living. In this way, the living relationship between people and law would once again be reestablished and the present split between the rigidity of the traditional requirements and the flexibility of modern Jewish living would be bridged.

Understood this way, the secret of Jewish survival is now clear. The Jews continue from generation to generation not as bearers of an idea of God or some other such spiritual theory but as a people. The folk endures though its culture changes. So there can be confidence it will survive the present age of transition. The Jews may adopt many of the ideas of their society, but as long as they remain a healthy and self-affirming people they will express these ideas in their own Jewish civilizational form. Not the content of Judaism, but its social base is what has and what will continue to give it identity.

One might have thought the post World War II "return to religion" and its accompanying intellectual emphasis on faith might have caused a major readjustment in this approach. It has not. Kaplan was among the sharpest critics of the so-called return, pointing out in substantiation of his social approach that it represented more a need to belong than a response of belief. As religion it did not go very deep and until there is a reconstruction of Jewish theology is unlikely to do so. Worse, as an expression of solidarity with the Jewish people it has taken an inappropriate because a too church-oriented direction.

Nor is the current interest in existentialism a reason to substitute it for naturalism as the philosophic context of a truly modern Jewish thought. Kaplan criticizes existentialism as a typical "failure of nerve." Men have, for the moment, lost faith in themselves and their capacity, and thus naturalism, which is founded on that faith, has seemed less appealing than irrationalist philosophies. But Kaplan remains confident that this mood will pass and naturalism will once again be seen as the handmaid of modernity.

Yet this postwar concern with religion has had its own effect upon Kaplan, perhaps more as a matter of emphasis than as a change in direction. On the surface it may be detected in his increasing concern with personal faith and commitment; one is not surprised to find the word "existential" repeatedly recurring in his writings. He has also increasingly emphasized that Judaism is properly a religious civilization rather than a folk civilization of which religion was but one, if the most significant, part.

One aspect of his social perspective could not help requiring serious restatement with the passage of time. The State of Israel was established in 1948. As a result of its subsequent growth and development, Kaplan's Zionism as a continuing ingredient of Jewish living looked to new horizons. Mostly he was disappointed in the general Israeli refusal to take the lead toward a reorientation of Jewish life as a whole. Zionism must exist for the welfare of all the Jewish people and not vice versa. To limit Zionism to support of the State is shortsighted, even disastrous. To argue that Zionism is focused on *aliyah*, "immigration," or the preparation for immigration, is harmful both to Zionism as a movement and to the morale of Jews who will not go to Israel. Thus he would like it made clear that the State of Israel is not really a "Jewish" state, nor is world Jewry properly described as a "nation." There is, rather, an Israeli State, while world Jewry is an international people, rooted in the Land of Israel but with branches everywhere.

Kaplan's criticism goes a step farther. If Zionism is not an end in itself but a means of enriching the life of the Jewish people, then the same problem of reconstructing Judaism affects the State of Israel as it does Diaspora Jewry. At the same time the possibilities of Jewish life in the Diaspora should not be negated. Reconstruction is more difficult there, particularly when seen in terms of a full-scale civilization, but is as possible off the Land as on the Land.

Time has not dealt kindly with Kaplan's social philosophy and its programs for Jewish community organization. There are no organic Jewish communities today, and it is increasingly unlikely in a day of rising congregational affiliation and importance that there will ever be any. Since World War II and the disappearance of immigrant communities the social drift in America has been away from distinct peoples to several religions, from cultural pluralism to religious diversity. Yet this has lent greater importance than he could have expected to his effort to rethink the ideas of the Jewish religion in naturalistic terms. Perhaps, ironically, the future will consider him more important as a theologian than as a social philosopher, for his point of view stands today as one of the few living theological options before the inquiring Jewish religious community.

The beginning of naturalist religious wisdom is the admission that the limits of the human mind prevent man from finally answering many questions: Who is man? What is death? Why is there evil? What are the limits of our freedom? Most important of all, reason cannot ultimately tell man what God is. To know him as he truly is, is impossible for one who cannot even understand himself. On all such metaphysical questions about God—his existence, his nature, his will—the only truly modern posture is agnosticism. Man, working from his own experience, from his world, simply cannot know.

That is why it is so important to distinguish between a belief in God and a conception of him. The belief precedes the conception. Faith is an intuitive response to the universe. Ideas of God follow. They are the cultural expression of that intuition. What is always involved in an idea of God may be socially understood. It shows man seeking to understand his world in a way that will allow him to live the fullest possible life. How God functions in man's life, not what He is in essence, is all man can know and as much as he needs to know about God. Faith in God is as important to man as is his effort to mature and grow. It is likewise indispensable, for it is part of his very nature to strive to be more than he is. Man's need for God, then, is a corollary of his necessary search for self, and belief in Him should then begin from man's best hopes and dreams. However, if man is to follow this inner drive, it must be based on an outer assurance, on realities which exist in nature. This is not to make an assertion about ultimate reality but to give a description of the religious man's attitude toward the world in which he finds himself. It is not a proof but only the expression of a fundamental intuition to say that since man's nature drives him to live abundantly, there must be a God to enable him to do so.

In what sense, then, does Kaplan use the word "God"? He rejects any description of Him as personal, for to him a personal God inevitably means an anthropomorphic one. This his naturalism finds intolerable. Some naturalists have therefore identified God with the strictly impersonal scientific concepts such as force or energy. Kaplan rejects this view too, for it is as untenable a metaphysical assertion as it is morally neutral. Put in its shortest form, Kaplan says, "God is the Power that makes for salvation." The assertion is remarkable. No other Jewish thinker has ever given a definition of God. Kaplan has done so not because he believes that this conception will describe Him in a metaphysical way but so that his basic religious intuition may be put into as rationally communicable a form as possible.

This God is not merely a fantasy but corresponds to processes and relations in nature which are undoubtedly real—all those which support man's efforts to live abundantly. So this sense that God is real comes not from some effort to comprehend being itself but by identifying the realities in nature which correspond to man's religious needs. God is then subjective in that He expresses man's hope that he can fulfill himself, but is objective in that He corresponds to those factors in nature which make it possible for such ideals to be achieved.

Kaplan is undoubtedly right in speaking of his God as real in this special sense. What should not then be assumed is that because God is spoken of as real that he is a unity which is real. To the average mind, reality implies individual and distinct existence, hence metaphysics or ontology. Kaplan abets this possible misinterpretation by referring to God in terms that seem to describe him as an entity. He is the Power, the Process, the Force, with both the article and the capitalization befitting a proper noun. However, that is not an accurate understanding of his theology. The unity of God to Kaplan is not a description of His being but of man's way of looking at Him. The unity is in man's language and reflects the consistency of his response to the universe. In its objective, "real" sense, the term "God" refers not to one integrated reality, but to many different forces in nature, to disparate objective realities. Kaplan never argues or asserts that there is any real unity among them. So when man thinks of the reality to which the term "God" is applied, the term "one" is inaccurate. Thus it is fair to say that for Kaplan, insofar as God is objectively real, he is not one, and insofar as he is one, he is not real. That two-leveled approach to the reality of the God which Jews assert to be One has made it difficult for many to accept Kaplan's conception of God.

A second problem is raised on the level of function. Granted that one can accept the reality of this God, he is understood to be fully impersonal. That is a great victory over anthropomorphism, but can an impersonal God have a personal effect on man? Can man take personally an impersonal God? Indeed, what happens to man's standard and ideal when God is impersonal? Should man give up his fight to be a person and instead model himself after the impersonal? Or is this but the most obvious case of the basic error here, defining God in terms of man's need rather than vice versa? From man's side an impersonal religion is a contradiction in terms. Religion either touches all one's heart, one's soul, and one's might, or it is nothing. Kaplan does not see why this should be a problem. People take their country very seriously. They address it personally and speak of it with deep affection. They will even give their lives for it. God conceived as the "Power that makes for salvation" is no more impersonal than one's country. Being far more closely involved in man's existence, He should be even easier to relate to personally.

Kaplan's rebuttals have not been convincing to many, including his own followers who themselves from time to time raise the issue of personal religion with an impersonal God. One wonders how it could be otherwise with any religious approach whose point of departure is science. The case of Teilhard de Chardin, currently in great vogue among Roman Catholics, is worth consideration in this regard.

Teilhard's effort to link science and religion was founded on his lifelong work as a geologist and paleontologist, as well as his general interest in the evolution of later biological forms. Teilhard claims, from a strictly scientific point of view, to see a direction in evolution and one which is unitive and constructive. Modern science leads him to the insight that the world is a continuous genesis, a steady becoming from the tiniest energy packets to very large molecules (cosmogenesis) which eventually, and astonishingly, produces life (biogenesis). Living things, too, are involved in a process of becoming and, in turn, unexpectedly produce beings which reflect and think (noogenesis). These now are evolving a new level of existence through sharing jointly in the universal life of the human spirit. This would be the convergence of mankind's spirit at the Omega point toward which the whole evolutionary process moves (Christogenesis). Teilhard escapes the impersonality of Kaplan's God by arguing that the Omega exists in itself and is supremely personal. The corollary assertion, required to maintain the unity of evolution, is that life is inherent at even the supposedly material level of creation, though it emerges clearly only on the biological.

Setting aside what some critics consider Teilhard's problems with Catholic dogma, his reconciliation of science and religion results in something more like what Judaism and Christianity have traditionally taught than does Kaplan's "Power that makes for salvation." Yet the mediator still finds severe critics on both sides. The scientists are the more biting. They argue that the legitimate interpretation of the meaning implicit in the discoveries of science should be limited to the methodological premises of scientific investigation itself. They reject the introduction of any sort of teleology, more technically, Aristotelian finality, or some other major change in contemporary canons of scientific interpretation. Yet without some such shift it is difficult to see how one could reason to the existence of God or of the reasonableness of faith in him. Efforts to vivify matter, to personalize reality, to add God by way of a little imagination, go far beyond what most philosophers of science can accept—and if that is the reception he receives among those whose approbation he sought to the extent of abandoning more comfortable categories of thought, why should he risk alienating the religious? For they will argue, as they have against Teilhard's personalist God, that he has been robbed of his transcendence and no place has been left for what was once central to faith, his mighty acts in history. The religious criticism of an impersonal God would only have been much more severe.

With science as the fundamental reference of theology, the dangers of immanentism seem unavoidable. That is in part the appeal of Whitehead and his current revival via Hartshorne in Protestant theology. There a metaphysics appears but has little appeal to the scientist as scientist, while its impersonalism and abstraction once again become a substantial problem for the religious. Obviously, religion cannot ignore any approach that might hope to bridge the great gap between it and science. Yet the key issue of the postatomic age is not the reality of science but the validation of persons. Any point of view which cannot on a quite fundamental level affirm persons cannot hope to be adequate to the most pressing question of this troubled era.

Some therefore declare that it would be simpler to abandon God or any term or attitude with similar reference and instead devote oneself to ethical living. But how can man escape Him or his surrogate? The ethical life for Kaplan inevitably involves faith and thus a relation to what Kaplan would call God. Man's ethical concern rests upon his self-transcendence. Duty speaks of other men, of society, of a world in which the ethical imperatives may become the reality of existence. Taking ethics seriously therefore means acknowledging faith in other men in a world in which it is possible to carry out those responsibilities. Such faith to Kaplan is what the religious man means by God. The ethical man already has it, but in religion through its idea of God and its sancta this intuition is clothed with a unique dynamic.

Kaplan's naturalism begets a reinterpretation not only of the idea of God but of all the major themes of Judaism. Here his approach to the problem of evil, prayer, the chosenness of Israel, and Jewish law will be briefly described.

Kaplan's theodicy is kept thoroughly rational by again substituting function for metaphysics. He will not say that he believes in a finite, a limited God, perhaps because this smacks too much of metaphysical assertiveness. Still, he does not refrain from limiting God to certain powers in the universe when he defines Him. God is not in all of nature, but only to be associated with those powers which make for man's self-realization. To declare flatly that this God is finite would resolve intellectually the problem of evil, but Kaplan rarely deals with it on this level. He is far more concerned with how to meet evil. The real problem is that it may deprive men of the will to better themselves or their world. Regardless of all the intellectual and emotional problems involved, man must find sufficient faith in the positive aspects of self and nature to continue to fulfill himself and thus transcend evil.

This consistent application of his view of God is likewise found in his treatment of prayer. It says far more about the worshiper than it does about the nature or will of God. Kaplan states boldly: "All thinking—and prayer is a form of thought—is essentially a dialogue between our purely individual egocentric self and our self as representing a process that goes on beyond us . . . when we wish to establish contact with the Process that makes for human salvation, we can do so only by an appeal to the higher self that represents the working of that Process in us. From that . . . we seek the answer to prayer." One prays then, so to speak, to oneself but to oneself as a place of consciousness of the realities which cooperate with Him whom man calls God. Why, then, will man pray? Because his nature as a self-transcending creature will always lead him to such inner reflection and aspiration toward a goal for his growth.

All this has been said as if prayer were a purely personal matter. Kaplan, of course, stresses it as a social act. Communal worship is not only an aid, it is a positive relief from private prayer. Here the group supplies perspective, channel, and incentive. No wonder then that the great religions have always advocated both solitary meditation and institutional services.

The practical effect of this view is of interest. Kaplan has led some of his disciples in preparing various prayer books, which are largely traditional but which show a number of theologically required omissions as well as some creative additions. This effort has not met with much success, certainly not more than that gained by the other American Jewish groups which Kaplan has roundly criticized. Indeed, the problem seems to have become exacerbated by this supposedly acceptable liturgy, for if one cannot pray it, perhaps one cannot pray at all. From time to time one hears from Kaplan or one of his disciples a suggestion for more radical change, generally an effort to give study the place previously held by prayer.

Neither Kaplan's view of evil nor of prayer has called forth as much controversy as has his attitude toward the concept of the chosen people. He has vigorously opposed it and has not hesitated to call it an immoral, divisive, arrogant idea. He has asked for its complete renunciation by the Jewish people. Chosenness may, at its best, have once meant moral responsibility and a challenge to the Jew. As the centuries have passed, it has become an assertion, even if unconscious, of Jewish superiority. It must be rejected by every modern Jew as generating hatred or at least suspicion between Jew and non-Jew.

Besides, the idea that God chooses a people is today as meaningless as the idea that God has some sort of conscious, personal will. The study of comparative religion has demonstrated the falsity of claims to exclusive revelation by the inconsistency of the doctrines asserted to be the only truth. The higher ethics of the contemporary world, with their universal horizon, make such tribalistic notions unthinkable.

Any religion that is genuinely interested in the brotherhood of man should formally renounce any particularistic doctrine of salvation. Kaplan specifically calls upon the Jews who have suffered so much from those who have held such ideas, and whose civilization has been permeated by their ethical concern, to take the lead in this direction. A sense of special communal purpose might indeed offer added inducement for Jewish living. It should, however, come as an open decision of the Jewish people, eager to serve mankind as well as its own members, not disguised as a supernatural act of God. Let the Jews choose a vocation. Since too often in the modern world nationhood has meant chauvinism, exemplifying the moral potentialities of nationhood could be a worthy vocation for the Jews today and make an extraordinarily important contribution to mankind.

A similar liberalism pervades Kaplan's attitude toward Jewish law. He does not wish to dispense with it but he feels the law must serve the people, not the people serve the institution of the law. He would modernize it by making it entirely voluntaristic. He rejects any sense of compulsion, either heavenly or human. He is rather desirous that variety and difference now become an accepted part of Jewish religious life. Positively, he would first wish to win the loyalty of the individual Jew to his people so that he will want increasingly to give his life Jewish identity and Jewish expression. Then by making Jewish practice as relevant and meaningful to modern Jews as possible, he believes many can be won to faithful Jewish observance. He would see this process most properly carried out by a democratic assembly of the organic Jewish communities he envisages, and hopes that because these would now be folk decisions they would carry special weight with all loyal Jews.

Kaplan has maintained this position consistently even though the Conservative movement as a whole has sought rather to move in a more traditional direction and develop what it calls "Law and Standards." Though he may have lost the struggle to guide the Conservative movement, it is difficult to say that he has not won his point about the impracticality of trying to have law as law and of the consequent folly of limiting official changes to what the processes of the law can be made to allow. His voice has regularly been raised in protest against the Conservative movement pointing out that the development of new patterns of practice has been insignificant. The lag of new law behind current problems is incredible if one is expected to take Jewish law seriously.

In sum, Kaplan has sought the most all-embracing framework for his Judaism. Not for him the parochialism of those who must preserve their childhood faith at any cost. All of man's history, all of his social experience, all of his knowledge of self and its development, must serve as the context of his Judaism. His own proposals refuse to be limited to one or another area of Jewish life. The whole Jewish people and the total spectrum of its existence are his concern. This has required him to adopt positions previously unknown to Jewish thought and caused him to take many an unpopular stand. He has not hesitated to do so. This integrity to principle, this courage of commitment, are admirably present in all his exposition.

Yet it is Mordecai Kaplan, the person, who has been his most extraordinary creation. The seriousness and formality of his writings generally mask his warm and lovable nature. The man himself is present, giving, open. He is that modern rarity, a real human being—and rarer still, an authentic modern Jew. His terms may be the terms of naturalism, but the tones are the tones of Sinai.

This praise is not meant to excuse his faults. It is simply his due. Yet, having shown what naturalism might make of Judaism, he has while bequeathing much to another generation clarified for them why they must seek another theological method.

Kaplan tries to start from a universal understanding of man

and society and from this justify the continuation of Jewish life in particular. He does that because of his confidence in the superior truth of that general understanding to Judaism, not only because it is modern and scientific but because it is more abstract. That judgment is, however, open to question. Is not all human truth inevitably particular and would not the truth about man be found more in particular men than in ideas about them? Thus the greatest truth man can know about religion is found in particular religions rather than in abstract theories about them. Instead of using modern concepts to teach Judaism what it is, Judaism should equally be the basis of judging the value of modern thought. Even in a partnership, Judaism would be a full-fledged judge and critic, not just a social channel or costume for the ideas of the age. To make this question more concrete, Kaplan believes modern science tells religion its role in personal and social existence. That is an extraordinarily high faith to place in an enterprise which has succeeded brilliantly in its understanding of matter and in its harnessing of energy but which disclaims knowledge of the realm of the spirit and prides itself on being ethically neutral. Indeed, that very value-free attitude, widely disseminated, has become one of the great human dangers of the age. One might then well argue today that science itself needs religion, including Judaism, to provide it with an independent, value-oriented view of what should be done with its increasingly powerful discoveries.

Moreover, is science the only model for modern man's thought? For Kaplan the intellectual choice is simple. One is either a naturalist or a supernaturalist. In the thirties that might have been obvious. Since World War II, however, naturalism has had a serious decline. Alternative methods, avoiding both possibilities, have since come to the fore, notably religious existentialism. One may well ask if either Buber's "Eternal Thou" or Tillich's "Being-itself" is natural or supernatural. Surely they are neither and both. Both men are hardly supernaturalists. Neither believes in miracles or in verbal revelation. Yet both can ascribe to God a unity far less subjective and far more personal than that of Kaplan. If the fundamental problem of modern man is how, in a technological age, to be and stay a person, then the existential, not the scientific, style of thinking is more responsive to modern man's experience. Moreover, it is an understanding of truth far more congenial to the truths that religion has traditionally sought to impart. From a social perspective alone, it is clear that one can be modern and be an existentialist and far more recognizable in one's Jewish faith as well. Kaplan's dogmatic insistence upon naturalism seems scarcely less than arbitrary.

Time has also raised serious questions about the natural necessity of life as self-fulfillment. The rising generation has seen too many men live by this illusion and because they were in the race to win, lose their freedom and integrity. The young are determined to be realists. Most lives are unfulfilled. With real goals infinite, what else is possible? Hope for self-validation through accomplishment or activity is an illusion they are ready to live without. Camus has taught them the world is, at best, benignly indifferent to human striving. They may try to be decent, but they prefer to play it cool.

For Kaplan such a position is inconceivable—but it is far closer to the realities by which post World War II man lives than any other. Kaplan's rejoinder only makes his position less believable. He would insist that science has discovered certain truths about human and social nature which are unchangeable. He seems to substitute a necessity arising from the workings of nature itself for the metaphysical necessity of older philosophies. The basic errors in this argument are contained in the assumption that what science describes as man's patterns in the past are what man must or ought to do in the future. The "must" ignores man's freedom. Once man knows the way in which social forces have operated, he has the possibility, if he chooses, of using his freedom to act against them. The "ought" case is the famous moral fallacy that illicitly seeks to derive an imperative for what it is right to do from a description of what, as a matter of fact, is. Perhaps in a world desperately in need of internationalism, separate, secular peoples are an anachronism that should ever more quickly disappear.

Besides, Kaplan's reliance upon social science was based on its earliest modern discoveries, those of Durkheim and Sumner. Much of what he accepted as permanent truth, where it is not rejected altogether, is now but one theory among many others. Thus though Kaplan often insists that science demonstrates a constant nature in individuals and society, modern writers rarely speak in such terms. His claims on behalf of the reliability and consistency of the social sciences are rarely heard among the practitioners themselves.

The entire Kaplanian discussion of human nature is dominated by the term "self-fulfillment" as if its meaning were self-evident. Surely man's self is not an entity in him. But if it is only a potential, how shall he know which of his various drives and powers lead to fulfillment? Without a standard external to his conflicted self, how can he ever know what fulfillment might be? And if God is interpreted in terms of man's self-realization, He not only cannot serve that role, but it is not clear what in man or nature He now might be.

All these questions concerning his general method would have their effect upon his theory of Judaism, yet a few specific comments of the many that could be raised are in order. The two-civilizations theory is particularly unappealing today. If the American people ought to develop its own religion, why should not the Jews give their energy to developing America's faith and thus end the anomaly of their minority status? It will not do to say every people ought to survive, because Jewish existence can lead to persecution of a kind unknown to any other people. If its disabilities can be that great, then unless there is an equally positive reason for remaining Jewish, there would be positive moral reason to rid the world of this dangerous social status.

If the Jews are really primarily a folk like every other folk, then their secular activities must be judged of equal worth to Judaism as their religious activities. But is Jewish folk dancing the Jewish equivalent of study of the sacred books? Is that greatest of contemporary Jewish folk acts, gossiping over coffee after services, really more important than the worship in which they rarely get or create an equal folk feeling? It is one thing to fear that Judaism as a "religion" may lead to the loss of ethnicity. It is another to say that religion is the first of many important folk involvements. Here Kaplan has, but in a form different from that which he used, made his point. It is difficult to believe that future Jewish theologies will not acknowledge the Jews as a people rather than as something like a church.

Two theological criticisms must be raised beyond what has been noted above. What once made God function in people's lives was their firm conviction, conscious or unconscious, that he was real. How can God function today amidst all men's realism when this unity is mental and his reality is plural rather than somehow an identity in itself? To argue from man's need for a God is already to lose the case. Of course, modern man would like to believe in God and believe that his efforts to live abundantly are supported by that God. Having been trained to ruthless realism by Feuerbach and Freud, his root question is whether there is indeed such a God. Only when he can affirm this, only when he is convinced that God is real, and is not just a prop created to spur man's morality, will he serve Him. Hence, functionalism cannot serve as a means of avoiding the metaphysical issue.

A word is in order, too, concerning the concept of the chosen people. That idea in its historical development is badly maligned by Kaplan. Rarely has a concept been as carefully hedged about by moral considerations as that one from the prophetic insistence that it did not supervene God's justice to the rabbis' careful explanation that it meant getting and doing commandments. Jewish "superiority" to others was, when it occurred in the past, and more clearly in the present, the response to the persecutor, not a product of Jewish theology. The changing social situation has already obliterated what there was of this attitude among Jews. Giving up a doctrine is no way to change social realities and bargaining with other faiths is certainly no reason to give up a religious belief. The truth of Jewish chosenness is not directly related to what Roman Catholics will do with salvation outside the church. It must be decided in terms of its intrinsic merit. The dangers of dealing with religious truth in a social context were never made more clear than at this point.

One might therefore be inclined to minimize Kaplan's lasting contribution to modern Jewish thought. His legitimization of a secularized Jewishness enabled many postimmigrant Jews to integrate into American culture while retaining some Jewish self-respect. When religion was on the defensive from a metaphysically imperialistic science, he created a theology in which a deanthropomorphized God could be understood in terms of the needs of men. What cannot be forgotten is that in a troubled and confused age, Mordecai Kaplan had the daring and capacity to seek out his people's problems and propose solutions to them which challenged the will and the intelligence of all who cared about the Jews. In so doing, he set an example in spirit and enterprise, if not in method and content, for all modern Jewish thinkers.

6

MARTIN BUBER: THE LURE OF RELIGIOUS EXISTENTIALISM

MARTIN BUBER published *I and Thou* in 1923 when many of the seminal religious works of the twentieth century were seeing light. By contrasting the paths their authors took with the one Buber pioneered for himself one may best appreciate his unique contribution to contemporary religious thought.

The problem of that post World War I era was, as in many ways it remains today, the justification of value. The war had been a dramatic, practical demonstration of what philosophy, in the person of its mad prophet, Friedrich Nietzsche, had known for decades. The old value systems were dead. Philosophical idealism could not survive the insight that rationality might essentially be a function of will or self and the old, naïve trust in class, caste, custom, party, or institution seemed absurd in view of what society did with persons. Nietzsche's own postidealistic experimentation seemed to lead only to anarchy or even worse under his sister's willful perversion of his manuscripts. Was there any way philosophically to save man's nobility, the life of the spirit?

Rudolf Otto charted one significant road in 1917 in *The Idea of the Holy*. It was a brilliant effort to retain the best of the German romantic spirit, expressed in religion nearly a century before by Schleiermacher and since lost in the vagaries of sentimentality and emotionalism. Otto's careful analysis sought to show that there was what might be called an "empirical" basis for religion, that man in full subjectivity senses the noumenal in the universe and this religious experiencing produces religion. Yet as the century's subjective aberrations progressed and the attacks of psychoanalysis from within and cultural anthropology from without gained momentum, what once seemed a clear and distinct idea was more readily understood as rationalization or illusion. Despite Otto's careful conceptualization, Romanticism refused to be shackled. The emphasis upon experience became a pretense for courageous research into overwhelming emotion, currently manifested in a growing preference for LSD to liturgy.

That is why the major energies of this period sought refuge in the certainty which science seemed to afford. Kant's dichotomy remained, but the noumenal was substantially abandoned to the phenomenal world, and an effort made somehow to find value, in a decidedly non-Kantian way, by extrapolation from what science was ever more successfully revealing. Lloyd Morgan, whose *Emergent Evolution* was published in 1923, sought religion by inference from the qualitative leaps which the concept of evolution had to postulate in order to describe the various levels of natural development. Teilhard de Chardin, had gone so far along these lines in his own distinctive way that in 1926, probably as a result of some lectures previously given, he was officially barred from publishing anything save strictly scientific works, thus explaining the hybrid intellectual form in which this loyal son of the church continued to express himself. At the same time Alfred North Whitehead, far more epistemologically oriented, was seeking to demonstrate that in the very way science cognizes, certain metaphysical assumptions are involved which lead one to postulate a grounding reality to all existence. These paths remain living options and when the sensationalism of the "death of God" discussion is over, theologians may have to come back to these men if they would speak religiously to the secular mind and mediate between science and religion.

Still, to many religious men there remains a fatal flaw in this theologizing out of science. At best it recreates God in a scientific image, cosmic and universal but impersonal and generally finite. The philosopher has a neat picture; the religious man does not know what to do with his piety. To love with all one's heart and soul and might that which is unconscious of and personally unconcerned with one seems perverse, even demeaning. When mathematical ideals become society's standard of value, the personal in man is bound to disappear, as the continuing dehumanization of man in technical cultures today testifies.

Hence, the would-be mediators were attacked from both sides. The rationalists found them going beyond the competence of their mental instrument and the religious men found them compromising authentic faith. Philosophers on the whole, represented most characteristically by Wittgenstein whose *Tractatus* was published in 1922, turned away from man and from those of his problems which would not lend themselves to strict conceptualization. They now limited their legitimate domain to analytic linguistic constructions or the philosophy of science, areas where they could be technically sound if humanly irrelevant. Mind had won a domain in which it could once more be master, but the price of this professionalization was academic solipsism. Professors could talk only to certain other professors, and at that, hardly about the love of wisdom about life.

Martin Heidegger remains unique among the creative philosophers of our day because he rejected the scientific model of certainty for philosophy without succumbing to the old ills of idealistic speculation. Turning his gaze toward man, he began the phenomenological investigation of the structures of being disclosed in him. Since the publication of *Being and Time* in 1927, Heidegger's analysis of man has had a continuing fascination for religious thinkers. Because Heidegger has focused his attention on Being, much of his writing has sounded like secular theology. But as he has become more elemental, his methodology has become inaccessible and his conclusions seemingly more capricious, an unforgivable development in a thinker who supported the Nazis with enthusiasm. He may have defended the autonomy of philosophic reason against science, but it is not clear that he has escaped the perils of anarchic willfulness which Nietzsche proclaimed as the next stage of philosophical speculation.

From the other, the religious side, Karl Barth, in Christ's name, rejected the hegemony of both scientific thinking and philosophical systems. Christianity might use one or the other to explain itself to men, but its first duty was to be true to the Christ. Its vocation, almost lost in an age of overeager liberalism, must remain authenticity not acceptability. In 1922, Barth issued the revision of his classic commentary on the *Epistle to the Romans*. Here his own unique vision, which had been crystallizing in the first edition, found coherent focus for the first time. Barth had discovered the human mind's inevitable inadequacy to God, God's nature, God's purpose. The divine transcendence was complete and any philosophy or theology that sought to confine it to humanly intelligible limits was idolatrous. It sought to subject God's essence to man's mind, to make man's logos the measure of God's being. Every effort really to know God by rising up to him from the human side must be spurned, but with openness men might yet receive what God once offered them and continues to offer them, a saving knowledge of himself through Jesus Christ. God's gift, his self-disclosure, the Christ, his Logos, must be the standard of man's understanding, and thus man's hope, consolation, judge, spur, and salvation.

Barth remains the prophet of authenticity to any man who would speak of his faith. In whose name does he speak and what is the authority behind his teaching? Barth seeks to let the Holy Spirit speak through him by loyalty to the Christ only. He is clearly a Christian. May the same truly be said of existentialist, ontological, or "death of God" interpreters of

Christianity? How can apologetic theology of any religion guard against compromising and perverting its traditional faith?

Yet, however magnificent is Barth's unexpected challenge from the divine side in a world intoxicated with technological triumphs, his is the triumph of dogmatics. Many religious men, particularly Jews, do not know Jesus as the Son, nor despite their openness, do they see why they should recognize him as such.

Barth does not, cannot, seek to validate his faith in common terms where most modern men should like some sense of personal and universal access to God.

The philosophical and religious independence of science which both Heidegger and Barth insisted upon was in this period practically confirmed by scientific work itself. Mathematics could no longer be considered an objective, eternal realm. Lobachevski's demonstration of the subjectivity of geometry had just been given empirical significance by the testing of Einstein's theories, and by 1931, Gödel was to produce his famous proof that all mathematical systems, which include cardinal numbers, rest in effect on some sort of faith. On the level of research, limits were also being reached. Planck's thesis of an ultimately spontaneous, subatomic world of energy quanta came to an intellectual climax with Heisenberg's publications on the principle of uncertainty in 1927. Science as the source of certainty might still be meaningful on the aspirin, or satellite, level, but it was not metaphysics; its foundations were not secure enough for it to be the criterion of religious truth. To the contrary, though it took an atomic bomb to demonstrate it, science itself is in need of an independent wisdom to counsel it where human goals and purposes are involved.

Martin Buber followed none of these views but single-mindedly pursued a vision original to himself. His genius was to integrate the objective and subjective approaches to reality into a dynamic, yet balanced, pattern. Perhaps his accomplishment may be epitomized best in this way: Buber found a way to limit the totalitarian aspirations of technical reason, with its subordination of the personal to the impersonal, without at the same time denying its legitimacy and usefulness. Yet while asserting the personal as the primary category of human meaning, he was able to control its anarchic self-assertion by grounding its authentic appearance and self-recognition in faithfulness to another self. The Kantian dichotomy between noumenal and phenomenal worlds has been retained, yet radically revised. It has been refashioned in such a way that the religious man can explain how he knows the reality of God and the importance of man in a world which remains largely one of scientific description. Buber accomplishes this, without resorting to dogmatism or to special states of religious experience, by explicating a human situation which is available to all and part of everyday experience.

The first sentence of *I and Thou* gives us the basic tension of man's existence: "To man the world is twofold, in accordance with his two-fold attitude." His twofold attitudes are, of course, the famous categories *I-Thou* and *I-It*. Buber does not disparage the I-It world and its revelations because he values the I-Thou world higher. Man spends most of his life living in the I-It condition and, so to speak, it is here that he must await the I-Thou. To reject the I-It world, in effect, would mean to reject the possibility of the I-Thou, for man can affect its occurrence only by opening himself to it as he goes his I-It way. Moreover, the I-It reality can be hallowed by living in it in terms of the understanding and insight gained in the I-Thou. Since the I-Thou is necessarily fleeting and formless, the attitudes and acts and rules and institutions that men create in the world of the I-It can give a permanence and endurance to the I-Thou which it otherwise would not know. The sanctification of the I-It by the I-Thou is thus the fulfillment of the I-Thou for men who must live in both realms, though these I-It arrangements must always be recreated in terms of the living I-Thou.

Buber neither fights scientific investigation nor revels in the absurdity of the human condition. He can validate rationality precisely because he knows its bounds. The difficulty with technical reason today is its imperialism, an insistence that all human experience is subject to the canons of its sense of structure. Scientism is determined to transvalue the I-Thou into the I-It, dogmatizing that anything which cannot be explained in terms of I-It is not really known nor worthy of reliance.

The first of four major consequences of Buber's thought, then, is his adamant defense of the person, the individual, the singular self, in an age when economic pressures abet political purposes in utilizing technical intellect to reduce the individual to the more easily manipulated class, group, or category. Buber has not been alone in making the IBM card the most sinister symbol of our dehumanization. All the existentialists with their concern for person over mind, for self over against rules about selves, have been responsible for it. Yet the avidity with which Buber has been read and quoted in the past decade or more, although *I and Thou* has been available in English translation since 1937, indicates that he has somehow been our special mentor in this regard. His vocabulary above all others has enabled us to understand and articulate what happens as we confront our advisor, our boss, our lover, our colleague, our relative. Now we know why we feel so hurt so often, for while we sought the "Thou," they, despite the first names and other pretensions of concern, allowed us only the "It." Now we see how hollow most institutions, situations, people, are. At best they give us a little time, but what we really want is attention, the sort that makes possible the I-Thou.

That is the Buberian revolution in which the sensitive youngster and the idealistic adult of the sixties have enlisted. They act upon no rationalist ideology of human equality or economic analysis of oppressed classes. They simply know that what we do to Negroes and Puerto Ricans is to treat them like "Its." So they fight for civil rights, not for an abstract cause, but for persons; and it has a special appeal to them because they can do something about the underprivileged in a very personal way. And the same motivation spurs the current movement for peace. When even the Viet Cong and the Red Chinese must be seen as "Thous" (until they are shown to be as humanly depraved as Hitler), then individuals will feel the necessity, personally, to seek to hallow even *Realpolitik.* The peace marchers may be naïve, as the civil rights workers were once called, but in an age whose thrust consistently moves in the direction of interchangeable men living in quiescent conformity and thinking only what the consensus of opinions allows, the effort to assert the rights of the individual against depersonalization in work, play, school, or politics is the most critical, practical effort of our time. Buber, because he teaches us what man can find only in genuine dialogue, because he knows and loves man in a way that neither Sartre nor Heidegger nor Tillich can, is thus the true champion of the existentialist fight for the individual.

Buber's second great influence is in the field of religion. His analysis of our perception of reality has made it possible for the thoughtful man to accept his religious faith as an integral part of his being. Somehow modern culture, spurred on by the contemporary university, that church of secularism, has made it seem foolish—even unworthy—to have faith, much less to talk about it. The weak of mind or poor of nerve might need God, but no thoroughly intelligent man could consider religious assertions meaningful. The I-It demands to dominate, but the man of faith knows God is *Domine,* Master, Lord, King. Buber helps him to know that just as the I-It does not exhaust the truth of human relations, or even of his own reality as he has come to know it in dialogue, so there is another dimension of truth, that of the I-Thou. It speaks to man with the full legitimacy of the reality inherent in the universe. Furthermore, just as man knows that the intimations of the I-Thou are more significant for his existence than I-It social sciences, so he knows that his meetings with the Eternal Thou are the most valuable and trustworthy he can have for determining his life's direction.

Buber rejects the term "experience," in the sense of Schleiermacher and Otto, for this ultimate I-Thou relationship. He wants to make certain that we realize that knowing God is not an unusual, exceptional event characterized by tingles or tongues, overwhelming bliss or overcoming power. It may leave a residue of contentment and serenity even as it will almost certainly command the man of the encounter. Still, to measure significance by sensation is to misunderstand the I-Thou with God completely. It is as commonplace as coming from a chat with the sense that your companion is a real person, one whose depths you have been permitted to see in a way unknown to you heretofore. No gongs chimed. No birds chirped. Persons met—that is all, and everything. So it is with God. He, as most religious traditions know, is to be sought in the everyday, in the immediate, in the simple, even as the grace we are expected to say before we bite into our hamburger in some greasy diner should testify.

Moreover, that direct sense of God himself is abetted by the shadowy knowledge which accompanies all our genuine knowing of other people. For in every authentic confrontation the miracle of the transubstantiation of Its into Thous takes place. What is the dimension in which these persons meet? What is the ground or context that makes such an extraordinary happening possible? In their meeting, the persons dimly know they are accompanied by Him. Two people always meet as three, for God is with them, making them as persons, and their meeting, possible. The consequences of his presence as the guarantee and criterion of their proper personhood are full of the highest ethical implications for those who would live by the demands of the given personal situation.

How often have we, faithful to our modernity and sophistication, suppressed this knowledge of the Eternal Thou which we ourselves have had? How cleverly have we learned to ignore this personal truth because it somehow seemed incompatible with all that gave our era meaning? And so the natural knowledge of God common to all men was ruthlessly spurned, together with man's spontaneity at love, at play, at making things of beauty. Buber came to teach us that we need not be such hollow men, deprived of self and God alike. In establishing the category of the I-Thou, Buber made it possible for us once again to know that we know God and thus to affirm what we have believed but doubted because we could not find words with which to speak of it.

He helps us to understand, thirdly, that we must therefore speak of religious reality, even as of persons, in a language different from that of things. Discourse in the realm of I-It is distinguished by precision, logical progression, verifiability, and coherent structure. The usefulness of such language and the security it grants the user should not be allowed to imply that it is the only sort of meaningful discourse possible—that only information which can be coded in the I-It pattern is communicative (what Marshall McLuhan might in our world of electric communication call a "Gutenbergian pathology").

As soon as one knows that the most significant realities of life are those which transpire between persons, one knows that they do not occur in the I-It realm. The sort of discourse that takes place on the I-Thou level is, by I-It standards, an odd sort of discourse indeed. It conveys meaning not necessarily in orders or signs or gestures but simply in presence. Being there is its content: the person of the other in relation to our own is its substance (cf. McLuhan: "The medium is the message"). All deeds, memorials, or formulas derive their meaning from reference to such a moment. They are not the meeting itself and should never be confused with it. To read our marriage license, or in an older generation, our marriage contract, is not to understand the reality which now exists between us, even though that language will be the clearest and the most verifiable that can be offered concerning our new state. Yet if we are fortunate, when we reread the letters or poems or diary we wrote, perhaps even when we look at the pictures we took or the souvenirs we collected, we may again experience the I-Thou of those days—and so even may you, the outsider. I-Thou discourse is never things, not even the best of words, but anything may make it possible if one comes in openness. And he who participates in it, as in love, will know and hear and realize.

To put it another way, it should come as no surprise that we are inarticulate about God, that he and our knowledge of him cannot be translated into I-It terms. To do so would be to render God an It, a concise definition of idolatry. So to call for definitions, concepts, or proofs of God is to address him in an illegitimate dimension. One does not define persons but hopes to meet them. One does not prove persons, except by living with them. One cannot know persons, unless one can risk making oneself available. That is why those who place certainty above all else cannot love and therefore cannot really live. So it is with God, which is why it is entirely appropriate for us to be commanded to love him rather than to conceptualize his essence or demonstrate his existence.

Religious language is inevitably, then, as a species of poetry, an evocative rather than a descriptive tongue, a word world where the reader must supply what the author can only hint at. That is why the form of Buber's masterwork, *I and Thou,* is so strange, lacking table of contents, chapter headings, postulates, or even direct connections between succeeding paragraphs. Buber knows he cannot convey the reality of the I-Thou in I-It terms. He has, rather, written his lover's diary of the human situation; and you and I reading it may, if we are graced, experience through his writings what we have actually lived in our lives. For the same reason, writings about Buber are less effective than making friends with people—an observation that clarifies why the preacher's person is more important than any week's sermon, why his visit was deeply meaningful, though we cannot recall what he said or did. Exemplification, not subtlety, is the real test of the Buberian.

Fourthly, by means of this language, Buber is able to give new relevance to traditional religious categories. His liberalism is not an emasculation of piety but its reinvigoration. One of the great bugaboos of modern critics of religion has been anthropomorphic and anthropopathic language concerning God. The danger in such expressions is that they will be taken literally, thus offending what any intelligent soul must demand of a fully universal God. Buber clarifies how God can be known as supremely personal yet in a nonanthropomorphic manner. But this does not mean that Buber defines or describes God as person. Such metaphysical assertion would be typically inappropriate I-It language. Rather, he says in all consistency that what man knows in all personal certainty is that God lets himself be known as persons are known. That is the simple truth derived from encountering him. He is available as persons are available; our relationship to him, if it is to be described at all, is best described by what it seems to be an extension of: the two-sided, mutual relationship of persons.

No thoughtful man will confuse the descriptions of God given in the Bible or prayer book with the God who is met. They are obviously human efforts to put into words the overflow of the ineffable encounter. The Bible is thus not God's own words. He gives no words, but only his presence. It is entirely the work of men, which is why these several thousand years later we find some of its expressions strange. Yet it is sacred Scripture, and not just ancient documents, because of what happens to us when we read it, open not just to its social I-It but to its depth I-Thou. Then we recognize that it is an unparalleled record of genuine encounters with God, for the experience which prophets and people had may be relived today in reading their words. The Bible is truly revelation without its every word being revelatory.

"Sin" and "atonement," words often shunned by liberals, likewise take on new meaning through Buber's characterization. Every relationship imposes obligations upon those who participate in it. That is why we dodge most of the people who come before us. We cannot stand the burden of knowing them, for when we have formed a relationship, there are deeds that cannot stand within the context of what we have become to one another. Once they are done, the relationship cannot be the same. It is not just our error or mistake, but a transgression of the trust and meaning which arose between us. It is a sin, for it carries a special weight of guilt and shame.

To restore the relationship, we must make up for what we have done, perhaps by apology, perhaps by compensating goodness, perhaps by both. Only then, as the other in his love forgives us, are we once again what we were—perhaps more. That is what religion teaches about our relationship with God. Commandment is the consequence of relationship. Sin is not the violation of a rule but action inappropriate to our covenant. Atonement is the search for a restoration of relationship. Forgiveness is the fullness of his presence now that we have sought him in new purity.

Buber, in these as in so many other ways, fills the traditional concepts of religion with new power and thus makes possible a contemporary religious practice which is more pious than the older liberalism and more sophisticated than unrefurbished traditionalism.

In these four areas Buber has contributed to the understanding of religion in general, and that is why he appeals to Christians and to the vaguely religious as well as to Jews. That does not make him any less a Jewish religious thinker, for Judaism has always had this universal content. The book of Genesis does not begin with the first Hebrews but only arrives at their necessity after stating its view that God and man, through the covenants made with Adam and, more explicitly, with Noah, have a living relationship, though most men spurn it. Hence, Buber, in speaking of what all men may know of God and his requirements of them, speaks out of a long tradition of Jewish universalism, though he does so in his own special accent.

The difficulty with all such justifications of religion in general is that, by contrast, all particular religions seem tribal and parochial. That coincides nicely with the contemporary anti-institutional mood implicit in the affirmation of persons as primary; and many a reader has fallen in love with Buber because he seems to have justified private religiosity, the life of I-Thou, over against any group or institution. Buber does that, but he does far more. *I and Thou, Between Man and Man,* and *The Eclipse of God* may be characterized as works on the nature of religious living. So to speak, they deal with essence. But because Buber drives continually to the concrete, because he is, in fact, an existentialist, he too must ultimately turn to history, to man's actual experience with God in real time. Buber does that in his works dealing with the Bible.

This question of the validity of particular religions comes with special poignancy to the adherents of a minority faith. Being a Jew means shouldering special burdens in an essentially non-Jewish world. If the truth of religion is universal, why preserve the differentiating forms of one's faith, particularly when they entail special responsibilities and disabilities? Much of the current agitation in Protestantism over the alleged death of God is a reaction to Protestantism's new minority status, for there are many who see little justification for maintaining its separateness from the flow of educated, cultured, moral Americanism.

Buber knows that one cannot live as a universal man but only in some particularity. In his early Zionist writings he laid great stress on the importance of peoples and nations to individuals seeking fulfillment and to the development of human history in general. His writings of that First World War era seem today to have the overtones of racialism about them, but that is due more to the limited vocabulary of that time than to his own thinking, which increasingly subordinated the determined to the volitional elements of man's existence. To the last years of his life he spoke of God's addressing nations as well as single selves.

The story of real man, standing in real time, is then as much the story of peoples as it is of persons, though the two are inseparable, for peoples are ultimately individuals and possess no corporate soul of their own. That is why history, though it is largely concerned with the corporate, cannot simply be an I-It discipline. To reject its I-Thou dimension may be necessary for the practice of modern academic historical technology, but it will not disclose the genuinely human elements in mankind's experience. The issue is particularly pressing, since it applies to the category of qualitatively unique historical moments, those which are decisive for man's self-understanding and his sense of purpose in history. Modern history prefers gradual development and discovery to the unprecedented, transcendent breakthrough. Like all science, it wishes to reduce the I-Thou to the I-It for purposes of management. Since Buber knows that the I-Thou is real, he insists upon the category of the unique in history. He knows that man and God can meet in time and that such encounters may prove historically decisive.

To know what has really happened to man in his experience with the Eternal Thou, one must read the Bible, for that, as far as men can yet tell, is where he was first fully known. To read the Bible with I-It eyes, as is commonly done in so-called scientific study, may be of some antiquarian interest, but it is really a caricature of the Bible's content, the continued presence of the living God to individuals and to a people. Read with the openness that one brings to the I-Thou, the historic reality of this experience emerges.

Buber sees in the Covenant of Sinai, which is the climax of the exodus narrative, such a unique event in human history. Standing at the foot of the mountain, the raggle-taggle band of newly freed slaves, moved by the incredible experience of exodus from the house of bondage and led by a man of extraordinary vision, enters a Covenant with God himself. This is no mere ritual act of sacrifice and legislation, no manipulation of the mob to give it structure. True, rites and laws are set, and as a result of them a people, worthy of that title, emerges to seek its destiny. But all rests on the knowledge that this people, Israel, has faced and known the God of the Universe himself. For, in the strange and overpowering events of those months, this people had become open to the presence of the Eternal Thou operating in human history, in their history. Here at Sinai, corporately, in one great moment of recognition and acknowledgment, they, individually and collectively, bound themselves to that God. They pledged themselves, as a people, to be his people, to serve him in human history, to carry the knowledge of him in their midst and to exemplify it in their private and communal existence. Knowing that this was the God of all mankind, they therefore bound themselves to this service, his service, until all mankind would similarly recognize him and live in that knowledge.

If that was not all clear at Sinai, it became clear to the people of Israel as it entered upon history in its wilderness wanderings and then in its efforts to live under God's law on its land. Much of its education in the meaning of the Covenant came from suffering and chastisement. The Sinai-golden-calf-punishment-return cycle runs through much of the Bible. The genius of the Jewish people was not that it was inhumanly saintly but that it acknowledged the truth even when it hurt to hear it, that it was able to turn its chastisers into its heroes.

Buber tells that story in *Moses* and *The Prophetic Faith,* in *The Kingdom of God,* and contrasts it with Christianity in the moving study *Two Types of Faith.* Buber knows that Israel's Covenant with God is as alive and needed today as it has always been. Mankind stands as far as it has always been from appreciating the reality of the Eternal Thou and therefore learning to treat all men as "Thous" so that genuine community, the Messianic Age, can come into being. With all the forces of society moving in totalitarian and technopolitical directions, with all of history swept before it, Israel's stubborn loyalty to man through God is all the more desperately needed. And Christianity, despite the truth of its own variety of faith, mediated and indirect, essentially individual and not ethnic, as Israel's faith is direct and communal, has not superseded or made obsolete the Jewish people's special obligation. Buber's own lifelong devotion to his folk and the rebuilding of its homeland on the Land of Israel, his devoting his final years to his work on the Bible—all of these are eloquent personal testimony to his devotion, not to some abstract, universal search for personal piety, but to his personal commitment to Israel's particular historic destiny.

To the contemporary Jew, then, Buber offers uniqueness without superiority; pride without chauvinism; chosenness without arrogance; mission without fanaticism. By making Jewishness rest on Covenant relation rather than on tradition and law, he has won historic roots without inflexibility; group participation without violation of conscience; messianic hope despite personal reverses. In his hands a minority faith has become a major human enterprise; being a Jew has become a high calling.

By Jew and non-Jew alike, wherever religion is discussed today, Buber's name must be mentioned. But because modern theologians are all his debtors does not mean that they have had all their questions answered, even in terms of what he himself has said. One which relates to his contribution to philosophy of religion in general and another in reference to Judaism must be raised.

The customary criticism of Buber is that his category of the I-Thou is so imprecise that it conveys no useful structure to the man seeking for certainty. When it is applied to the area of ethical behavior, one of its apparently most significant uses, its subjectivity, would make possible the most horrible abuses.

The fanatic and the inquisitor regularly hear voices and have a sense of God's authorization. Is not reason man's only defense against the fiendishness made possible by man's self-delusion, operating under the guise of the I-Thou?

The problem is difficult indeed and made more troublesome by the fact that it is not academic in our generation. Yet the opposite truth must also be stated. The greatest evils of the day have been perpetrated not in the name of subjective improvisation but as a result of applying reason. Auschwitz and Hiroshima were deliberate and calculated triumphs of planning and philosophic argument. The same may be said of *apartheid* in South Africa, segregation in the South, and many of man's other most vicious practices toward his fellowman. Neither human reason nor human institutions are proof against man's talent for perversion. Buber could not deny the element of freedom and hence of risk in following the dictates of the I-Thou, but if one could indeed accept the other man as fully human and therefore bound to oneself in mutuality and responsibility, this would surely create a new and better climate of behavior. That is, of course, turning the I-Thou encounter into an I-It rule, which is illegitimate. And yet, though one cannot foreclose what the next encounter may demand, one must apply to the I-It world in its terms what remains of the I-Thou moments; and thus far, it has not been better expressed than in this love of persons. This is not a man-proof ethic, but it is far better than any other the age has yet known.

The far more interesting problem in Buber's universal thought is the unmentioned relationship between the realms of the I-It and the I-Thou. What unites them? What gives them their common ground? What makes it possible for man to live in both of them?

This dualism of Buber's is not merely an affront to that older type of philosophic mind which insisted dogmatically upon unity and structure. It is a very practical and consequential question as applied to God. When we know him in the realm of the I-Thou, we may know him to be the ground of all that is, the source and foundation of all existence. But we cannot know him that way in the world of I-It. He does not enter the world of the I-It, for he is, by definition, that which can never become It. And as long as we insist upon looking with I-It eyes, we never see him at all. Then how does he relate to the world of I-It? What is his place in that dimension of being in which we must spend most of our lives?

Two possible answers suggest themselves. The first is that the I-It world is not real but only man's construction. That first, decisive sentence of *I and Thou* seems already to make that point twice, first by beginning in emphatic construction with the words "To man" and second by reminding us that this is in accord with "his [man's] twofold attitude." Buber almost seems to continue the tradition of Kantian a priori categories of thought, except that he does not argue for the existence of necessary cognitive structures but, existentialistically, accepts what happens in the concrete human situation as best he can discern it.

Still, turning the I-It world into a projection of the human mind makes Buber an idealist philosopher, an appellation he would deplore and one that contrasts oddly with his insistent refusal to turn away from the concrete and immediate in the search for truth.

The other option is to argue that while the I-It world is real in and of itself, the I-Thou world is known to us as "more" real and hence its truth provides the greater context within which the I-It world must be comprehended. Buber often speaks this way as he discusses the importance of hallowing our day-to-day lives in the I-It world. But that is just what we do not understand. How can the Eternal Thou be related to a world in which He has no place and in which He is not seen? To put the question in more concrete cultural form, as science increasingly supplies mechanical or electrochemical explanations of phenomena, the natural world, the world of I-It, seems fully and finally closed against His entry. If that world has any reality, how does the Eternal God rule it, guide it, provide for it, or simply enter it to make the I-Thou possible?

Buber provides no answer to this question. Perhaps it would be better to say that this is not the sort of question which has meaning for him. For what it demands is a unifying intellectual perspective, usually an I-It view in which the I-Thou is to be comprehended. That attitude, for Buber, is the intellectual root of the eclipse of God today. Buber is satisfied, rather, to take man's strange dualistic situation as he finds it and learn to live with it in sanctity, instead of insisting on an understanding that he believes cannot ever be achieved. Whether modern man can stand such duality is a serious intellectual problem indeed.

The problematic character of the I-Thou is also at the heart of the particular Jewish issue that must be raised. It is related to the often mentioned matter of Buber's rejection of the validity of Jewish religious law which has played so central a role in the history of Judaism. In this attitude many scholars, particularly those of a more observant bent, have seen the basis of his lack of wide acceptance in the Jewish community.

The crux of the famous discussion between Martin Buber and Franz Rosenzweig on the binding quality of Jewish law hinges on the place of corporate experience in personal responsibility. Both men agree that religious reality is not to be found in an effort to live the life of universal religiosity but, for them, for other Jews, and for those who would join them, within the Jewish people and as part of its Covenant relationship with God. Both agree that as part of the Jewish people the individual has certain responsibilities to the group which are simultaneously responsibilities to himself, particularly study and personal appropriation of Jewish literature. Both agree that even where the individual himself sees no immediate meaning or significance to the text about to be studied he ought to open himself up to it and let it say to him what it may. Here discipline precedes meaning. Rosenzweig analogously urged such a standard with regard to Jewish law, that the individual should consider himself bound by it in principle and seek to do as much of it as he can. At this point Buber retreated, insisting that when it came to action as distinct from understanding, no criterion could be interposed between the I and the Eternal Thou. While the law might indeed serve to open the individual Jew to the presence of God, one could not in good conscience ask him, in advance, to enter upon an act he did not personally feel himself commanded to do.

At the heart of this stand is Buber's argument that the person, not the folk, is paramount when it comes to action. While he may choose to participate in this or that common pattern of Jewish religious activity, he should not feel himself obligated to do so in advance of a personally given sense of God's concern. Dialogue alone determines commandment.

Yet there is something of a problem if not an inconsistency in Buber in this area and on two levels.

The first concerns his certainty of the reality of Israel's Covenant. He knows it is a corporate reality and that it continues from generation to generation. He gives every indication of believing that it will so continue until the end of days. There would seem to be a sense, then, in which Israel's corporate religious destiny is distinct from the interests and decisions of individual Jews. That is, the Covenant apparently exists so surely that even if all Jews turned against it, it would still somehow survive. Or, what is the same thing, there is a providence that operates in history so that all Jews cannot ever totally reject the Covenant. If that is true, then there must be a level, somewhere, where the individual is not entirely the arbiter of what is and what shall be, and thus, particularly since it is the major means of expressing the reality of the Covenant, on the level of behavior as well. If the Covenant is a joint undertaking and its most significant articulation is in the way people live, then there must be communal and corporate forms of living it and not merely those which the individual at each moment spontaneously determines to do.

Buber might respond that such group practice should be the natural result of the practice of many individuals who stand in the same basic relation to God and who, by living together, will quite organically come to express this in common patterns. And while law and institutions may be necessary for any effort to carry on these insights over generations, they ought always to be subject to such individual, not corporate, needs.

Yet, is the real man of history, in this case, the Jew, simply the I of I-Thou? That is, is his Jewishness, his sharing in a corporate covenant, somehow not essential to his existence but only an accretion? If so, Jewishness should be as subject to judgment as every other social accident and so as often discarded as accepted. Yet Buber seems to argue that the crisis of modern Jewry is its refusal to accept its Jewishness, to identify the individual Jewish being with Israel's Covenant. Thus Jewishness is a matter of metaphysical reality and not an existential accident. But that means one's individual being has a corporate dimension as it shares personally in what is the people of Israel's Covenant. One can be true to oneself, therefore, only as one is true to that folk and there cannot be any distinction between the two. That may perhaps be a situation of great ambiguity and tension, and much of modern Jewish life is the struggle to integrate the warring parts of the Jewish soul. The issue of Jewish practice therefore cannot be reduced to what the disembodied I sees as it stands over against the Eternal Thou, but what the I/Jew, which must be true to group in order to be true to self, and vice versa, now knows itself to be called upon by God to do. That may not justify external law in and of itself but it makes common standards and patterns of practice necessary, for it rejects the radical split between personal and group activity, seeing them instead as two parts of one whole.

This is to say that I in an I-Thou relationship is substantially determined by his specific situation. Support for this inference is given in the unexpected, variant description Buber gives of the personal relationship between a teacher and his student. Obviously from Buber's point of view the good teacher will not confine himself to I-It competencies but will be concerned to help his student become a real person. He will find a way to engage him as a Thou. As Buber describes this in his essays, the reader cannot fail to recall the few teachers he has had who addressed him in this way and who may have brought him to interest in topics which previously seemed strange and alien. Good education is inevitably the evocation of the Thou. Yet Buber notes that in this process the teacher cannot go so far as to make himself fully present to the student. He cannot simply become his friend or companion, his Thou. He must always maintain a certain distance or he ceases being a teacher. Here the I-Thou relation is real but one-sided and not mutual. This account violates what we have heard about the I-Thou relationship, that it is characterized by full mutuality on both sides, that only as both persons are fully present, can I meet Thou. How would it then be possible for the teacher to evoke the student as Thou when he retreats at its approach and hides his own self? The answer must be found in the concept of situation or role. The teacher is not simply an abstract when he enters the classroom. He is there precisely as teacher and master. His self as self exists as teacher if he is real in that vocation. To be sure, he is more than a teacher and if he lives his entire life only in this restricted setting, he will be doing himself great harm. But, to borrow a Kabbalistic conception, he has constricted his full personality for the sake of accomplishing this important task, teaching the young or the old, and in the task he finds himself as self and not as It. Hence, when he addresses his student in his full person, as teacher, he may be said to be participating in the mutuality that makes a genuine I-Thou relationship possible. Perhaps this violates Buber's canon that in the I-Thou relationship the full person is present and known. If there is no room in Buber's understanding for the sense of persons being persons in specific situations rather than only in their fullness, it is impossible to know how he explains the reality of the student/teacher relation he so aptly describes.

The Jew, then, would be the man who stands athwart the Eternal Thou, not simply as universal self, but as Jew-self, individual and member of a people simultaneously. Hence his sense of relationship and of duty will always be as much a matter of folk as of self, of the Covenant of Sinai as of this particular moment.

This may pass beyond what Buber himself taught but it is what those whom Buber has made self-consciously believing Jews may now well learn from him. To those who feel that this shows no great respect for his unrelieved emphasis upon the individual in his discussions of Jewish practice, one may recite a story he told with obvious approval: When Rabbi Noah, the son of Rabbi Mordecai of Lekhovitz, assumed the succession after his father's death, his disciples noticed that there were a number of ways in which he did not conduct himself as his father had, and asked him about this. "I do just as my father did," he replied. "He did not imitate, and I do not imitate."

7

ABRAHAM JOSHUA HESCHEL AND JOSEPH BAER SOLOVEITCHIK: THE NEW ORTHODOXY

From the vantage point of classic Jewish faith Martin Buber may be adjudged the most Jewish of the liberal Jewish thinkers. His God, even without metaphysics, is real and personal, far more like the living God of traditional Judaism than any idea, mystery, or process could be. His sense of the people of Israel encompasses its rich nationality without in any way belittling or subordinating its relationship to God. In giving new meaning to the ancient sense of Covenant through his sensitivity to what happens in personal encounter and dialogue, he has reaffirmed the faith that lies at the center of Jewish being. Yet with all that, he is the least able of any of the liberal thinkers to validate Jewish law or substantiate communal standards of religious practice. Cohen knows ethics to be required; Baeck adds the obligations imposed by mystery and shared with a unique people; Kaplan makes the folk authoritative for all who are its healthy members. Buber in his strict individualism and insistence on the command of this hour is the most antinomian of them all. He acquires Jewish faith at the price of any rule or norm of Jewish practice. That is an inversion of classic Jewish thinking which gave precedence to action over belief if a conflict between them was unavoidable. Here again the flaw of the classic liberal strategy reasserts itself. Jewish reality is ordered by a superior modern truth, in this case, Buber's understanding of the I-Thou relationship. As a result, one of its fundamental aspects seems to have been lost or slighted. Wherever that has been felt in the past, the effort to create a contemporary Jewish theology has been resumed. So Baeck may be said to have gone beyond Cohen in order to restore a felt relationship with God. Kaplan added ethnicity and Buber reaffirmed the Covenant as a relationship between two living realities. Yet in taking modern Jews that far in belief, Buber makes the issue of Jewish practice so central that he in turn must be surpassed.

That is a necessity created not only by the reaffirmation of the Covenant but by the realities of Jewish social existence as well. If Jewishness became a personal, existential stance, though related to the Jewish people, it would be difficult to know what would keep the Jews as a group alive in the Diaspora. Buber seems to have known this. He writes very little about the possibility of Diaspora Jewishness. He was in life, as in theory, a Zionist. He could find in existence on the Land of Israel among other Jews a situation in which his radical individualism might not destroy the people he cherished. Diaspora Jews know, particularly because their community is relatively invisible, that the Jewish act is the fundamental sign and basic form of their peoplehood and the major means of fulfilling their relationship with God. Without communal practice of some kind there can be no meaningful existence for the Jewish people off the Land. The searching minority of American Jews who seek to reclaim Jewish religious existence know that sooner or later the critical issue is observance as part of the Covenant folk. They have come that far in their lives, so they seek a theology that will speak to their Jewish need. As long as liberal Jewish thought sets a secular criterion over Judaism it is difficult to see how their questions can ever receive a significant response, much less an answer. So what they require is a postliberal approach to Jewish theology.

That theological and social thrust lies behind the special interest in the two mature American Jewish thinkers, Abraham Joshua Heschel and Joseph Baer Soloveitchik. Both know and appreciate the contributions of the Jewish liberals, but both take a far more classic stand. The one is associated with the more traditional wing of Conservative Judaism. The other is as close to a spiritual leader as American Jewish Orthodoxy is likely to have. More important, both men have worked at creating an adequate theology of traditional Jewish faith. If the Jewish times call for a move beyond liberalistic theological methodologies, it is of the greatest importance to examine the position of these traditionalists.

Abraham Joshua Heschel is professor of Jewish ethics and mysticism at the Jewish Theological Seminary of America. That apparently odd combination of competencies reflects a biography and a career of the most varied religious interests. Scion of a distinguished Hasidic dynasty and as a youth deeply steeped in Jewish learning of the East European style, he won a doctorate from the University of Berlin with a phenomenological study of prophecy. A deeply pious person who was not shaken from his inherited faith by the move to the West or the university, he did many of his early studies on technical problems in medieval Jewish philosophy. A student of the history and development of Hasidism and one who shows the continuing influence of its emphasis on subjective piety, he has written his major books trying to set forth the intellectual structure of Jewish faith. A man who communicates the living possibility of mystical awareness, he has been the single most active Jewish religious thinker in such matters of social debate as civil rights, the Vietnam war, and the treatment of the Jews in the Soviet Union. More could be said but will not, yet one thing must be added. Born and early educated in Poland, trained to the modern academic style in Germany, forced to flee to England and then becoming an immigrant to the United States, he is a superb stylist in Yiddish, Hebrew, German,

English, and, it is said, Polish as well. He has published in all of those languages and, as will soon emerge, this brilliance at language is not merely a gift he exercises but a major method of communication for him.

Anyone who picks up one of Heschel's volumes is immediately struck by the unique quality of the writing. One can be so taken with it that one misses the cognitive development that is going on beneath it. That problem is increased by the way in which the idea structure is developed. Modern argument normally proceeds in linear fashion with one idea following another until a climax is reached in the major point the author is trying to make. Heschel does not proceed this way, but much as Buber did, with whom he was for a time associated in Germany. His sense of a reality apprehended in a nonempiric way makes him eschew in theological writing the form of discussion created by procedures of test and demonstration. His paragraphs may deal with one theme, but their sentences are not additive. He does not communicate cumulatively. Rather, his sentences tend to be radial, all centering about one motif but pointing to it or away from it in somewhat different ways. So, too, the paragraphs that combine to form a chapter are not joined in ladderlike progression to reach a new level of thought. They, too, generally aim at multiplying the insights and expanding the vision. Yet, unlike Buber, he is able to make a total structure emerge out of the sequence of his chapters, and it is this as well as the specific ideas which demands attention.

For Heschel there are three ways to full religious truth: through nature, revelation, and the holy deed. In the life of piety they are not separable, yet because of the social and intellectual situation of the modern world it is helpful to speak of them in turn and to recognize what each path lends to and borrows from the other two.

Were the term not so easily misunderstood, Heschel might be termed on the first, most generally available level, a nature mystic. That would be true in regard to his extraordinary sensitivity for the wonder that inheres in all things, for the hidden reality that the seemingly ordinary actually reveals. Yet it would be false to his sense of the normalcy of this sort of perception. He is not a believer in special states or special talents for religion. One does not need to be transported to other realms or achieve blissful identity with the infinite to know most intimately that God is announced everywhere and at all times. If anything, such a response to the universe is more natural than the skepticism that modern culture cultivates. That is why piety is normal to children and universal among primitives. Modern man has made himself unnatural by training himself not to be amazed, by working hard at not responding to the world in awe. That is the root affliction of an age anxious to the point of personal paralysis and moral incapacity. What men need most today is to recapture that radical amazement which is the most basic level of faith. They need to let themselves ask once again with full force and fervor: Why is there anything at all? Why is it so wondrous, so unexpected? Why is it men can even ask and marvel?

Here Heschel's felicity with images makes its most impressive display. He is addressing an audience dulled by the demythologization of nature and desensitized by sermons through science. Argument will not evoke awe, only another sort of technical rational understanding. So Heschel writes so as to illuminate, and like the great painters and photographers, he makes us see what we have seen a thousand times but never as truly as now. Had Heschel done no more than to remind men how the lens of faith brings a new depth of focus to the way one sees the world, he would have accomplished a major theological task. To have done so in an age which is so jaded to the amazement of existence that it had forgotten that nothing should be taken for granted can only be called healing.

Every theologian whose faith is ultimately connected with a specific religious tradition must come to terms with the truth of other religions, with religion as a universal human phenomenon. Heschel meets this problem at the natural piety level and that gives him a broad base from which to appreciate the variety of the religious experience among men. Yet his problem as a man of a given historical faith is that he must find a way, without denying his universalism, to establish his particular faith. For Cohen that is almost a matter of historic accident. In Baeck it becomes a matter of necessity for spirit in history. In Buber it is made more substantial by the God who does, as a matter of personal experience, appear when and where he wills. In Kaplan it is a matter of social form, but that in turn is a matter of natural necessity.

Heschel is too Jewish to be satisfied only with the universal God seen in nature and too traditional in his Judaism to accept one of the liberalistic validations of Jewish identity. The communal historic level never achieves the importance of the personal even in Kaplan's prescriptive sociology. Heschel, rather, adopts the classic Jewish stand, though typically he presents it in a fresh way. Existence reveals God, but as yet there is no speech, there are no words. That comes with direct revelation itself. The greatest miracle of creation is the Bible, where what was perceived mutely unexpectedly rises to the level of content-full communication. Man knows God more directly than in nature through the law of the Lord which is perfect and restores the soul. A creation-directed piety might be appreciative but it would be passive, relatively inert. In revelation, the God of majesty, power, and creativity becomes the commanding, responding God as well. Now a new type of religious understanding is born, one that can recognize the truth of the preceding layer but one that knows its limits and the direction of its fulfillment as well. Yet in the modern world, men can hardly be expected to perceive the truth of this second level if they are estranged from the first level. Then the Bible is another technical problem to them, a set of conundrums about literary sources, dates of editing, or compositions and literary types seen in social functioning. No wonder they cannot find God in it as did their fathers. With nature and their place in it now a question of mathematical interrelationships, the Bible has been rendered mute even before a conscious demythologization takes place. That is why Heschel felt the need to give so much time and effort to the most immediate level of religious insight, for as long as creation remains closed and sterile, not many men can appreciate the fuller truth of Biblical revelation. So Heschel's universal religious theory was stated first in *Man Is Not Alone* to make it possible in *God in Search of Man,* after its partial reiteration to move on to level two, and eventually level three. One may see here Heschel's interest in reaching out to modern man, the questioner, in an effort to help him find his way to Jewish faith.

The statement concerning Biblical revelation instantly raises the old liberal questions concerning the humanity of the Biblical text. Heschel is aware of all the problems of Biblical modernism. Some he proposes to meet by calling for an openness to what speaks through the text, the sort of religious sensitivity created by radical amazement. If this replaced scholarly detachment and critical hostility, many of the modern questions would simply not be there. More important, however, is his theory of revelation which is fully unique to him and represents an ingenious solution to the problem of a fully divine revelation cast in fully human form.

For Heschel, the prophet is in a special category, one which lies beyond that of even devoted religious men. His outstanding characteristic is what Heschel calls and carefully delimits as sympathy. The subjective overtones of that term are gratefully accepted as properly taking the prophet beyond cognitive enterprises or political planning. What grips the prophet is fundamentally existential, beyond technical patterns of analysis or explanation. He is in his ultimate depth fully turned toward God and sensitive to what is happening in the divine. Yet this is no abandoned subjectivity of wild emotionalism or cultivated irrationality. The prophet remains himself, possessed by sufficient will to respond to God and by sufficient individuality to make efforts to resist him or to argue with him.

Heschel is closer to Buber's theory of the I-Thou relationship as revelation than he is to any other thinker. Yet though he analyzes and differentiates himself from several dozen thinkers in this area, he cites Buber in his work on prophecy only as a historian of Biblical religion. His contrast of sympathy with the I-Thou experience would have been most helpful to the student of theology. Heschel seems to have three major differences with Buber. He claims a certain reflective or cognitive aspect to the prophet's experience which, if it is understood in the sense of sympathy, is well conveyed in the term "understanding." He also gives God a far greater place in the moment of prophetic sympathy than Buber seems to find in the I-Thou relationship. While the prophet is not overcome to the point of loss of self or union with divinity, it is nonetheless God, the one real Master of the Universe, he stands in relation to. How can what God is experiencing at this moment not become the overpowering, overcoming reality of such a moment? For it is not, as Buber says, just presence which the prophet experiences then and, so to speak, later fills in with his own words and content. Rather, Heschel understands the prophet, though expressing it in his own personal style and through the symbols of his culture to be giving an accurate, reliable account of what God is going through or demands at this moment. Heschel's position has, therefore, fairly been described as a sophisticated fundamentalism, one in which the Biblical text is taken as true to God's own reality yet without becoming involved in defending every word as God's own or every manuscript as a photocopy of God's dictation. Perhaps the differences from Buber are already implied in the fundamental phenomenon under discussion. Buber speaks of man's universal experience, as befits a liberal. Heschel, in more traditional religious fashion, reserves a special category for Biblical revelation and it is that which he discusses.

The corollary of this position is a defense of God as described by the prophets, namely, as a God who is known by man, not in his essence, but in his action and reaction to man. God is best described as a God of pathos, as one who, though there is an unbridgeable gap between him and man, is a God of feelings. The happiness, the sadness, the outrage, the determination the prophets ascribe to God are not only real but the most important things men need to know about God. Not essence, not even existence, but God's concerns are critical to men. In his historical and analytic attack on the notion of God as superior because unfeeling and in his elucidation of the meaning and human implication of the prophetic revelation of God as a God of pathos, Heschel shows the power of old religious categories to speak in new ways, and makes his own genius evident as well.

Christianity, perhaps even Islam, could join Judaism on the second level of religion, in faith as attentiveness to Biblical revelation, and Heschel is fully open to the areas of mutual concern and religious partnership which Judaism has with these traditions. He is a frequent participant in interreligious activities of both an intellectual and activist nature. Yet there comes a point at which he must assert the distinctiveness of the people of Israel in its relation to God. That comes about, though he is barely explicit concerning it, in a little-noticed aspect of his theory of revelation as well as in the third level of full religiosity. Traditional Judaism speaks not only of the revelation of the written Torah, the first five books of the Bible, and by extension all of it, but of the oral Torah as well. The writings of the rabbis and the rabbinic traditions down to this day are almost equally to be taken as having God's own authority behind them. The most significant practical consequences flow from that faith and divide the contemporary wings in Judaism. If the rabbinic tradition as applied by its chief spokesmen in the current generation speaks in God's name, then only such changes from the past as they authorize are authentic to Judaism. However, if the rabbinic tradition is essentially human in its authority, then its past decisions may be changed and its present proponents disagreed with if there is good reason for doing so. Heschel's position, with a proper concern for development and change, is the inseparability of the written from the oral tradition. He can say, "The prophets' inspirations and the sages' interpretations are equally important." That might make him Orthodox. It at least puts him at the right side of the Conservative movement and differentiates him from its liberals as well as from Reform Judaism. And it is clear that for Jews, the fulfillment of the Bible is the rabbis and not the Gospels or the Koran.

It is not altogether clear how that distinction works out on the third level, where God is met in the holy deed. Here Heschel produces a religious epistemology of doing the commandment which is very impressive. Modern students of religion are so accustomed to hearing about religious feeling or faith as it affects existence that it comes as something of an innovation to hear of the inner life of doing. Yet neither experience nor existence but commandment is the central concern of traditional Judaism. Heschel now describes not what brings man to a deed but rather what can happen to him in the risk of doing, in the leap of action. For in the fullness of a decision confirmed as it can be only in a deed, man more than becomes himself. He meets God. He knows himself to be responding not merely to his own desires but to God's. The final stage of human religiosity is learning to make God's needs man's own, to want to the point of continual doing what God wants.

That too, emphasis on works, would seem to be far more Jewish than Christian, yet it is not a clear-cut point of distinction. While Heschel continually speaks of *mitzvot,* of divine commandments and cites rabbinic sources liberally, he refers continually to man, not to the Jew, and his discussion on the Jewish people occupies not half a dozen full pages of his major works. He specifically states there that he is eager to set forth the universal human significance of classic Judaism. This third level then might be found in that understanding of Christianity which sees gospel as including if transcending law and which calls for a sense of genuine discipline and content to the Christian deed. That would not violate Heschel's own understanding of the inadequacy of the ethical as a sufficient category for religious acts, for Christianity too speaks of deeds as a response to God. Yet though this third way of coming to know God may have universal overtones, it seems clear that it is most fully expressed in the traditional Jewish life of law and commandment. Hence Judaism as a particular way of life is authorized by its continuing response to the revealing God which any man of universal faith now ought to be able to see.

For Heschel, then, the revelation to Israel is central, though he has mitigated something of such literalism as the Jewish tradition knew. This gives him so great a sense of the certainty of his position that he is led into two patterns of discussion which become extremely disturbing to one who does not share his faith or has some questions concerning it. Heschel regularly fails to see the validity of the questions that come from the other side, and he cannot appreciate even the possibility of alternative positions to his own. Again and again he begins with the discussion of a modern problem, shows its assumptions or its implications, and just as one expects that he will respond to these directly, he says, instead, that from the standpoint of faith that is not the real question at all. When one is fresh to this technique or when the insight is quite striking—religion is not man seeking God but God in search of man; the Bible is not man's theology but God's anthropology—the effect can be quite telling. Almost as with a Zen koan or a Hasidic master's epigram, enlightenment may strike. Yet the repeated exposure to that treatment, particularly in works that call themselves "philosophy," makes one increasingly uncomfortable. No one likes to have his questions ultimately dismissed as meaningless if not downright wrong, particularly when they are not individual whim but a product of the major intellects of the day. That unease increases to downright irritation when dismissal of the questions gives way to the rejection of alternate positions to the author's as simply "arrogant," "absurd," "insane," "incredible." They are not even considered, only anathematized. At the best, that says something about his passion for his own belief. He is so certain of his faith, alternatives are simply untenable. Yet again and again in the modern world, the unthinkable has turned out to be the more true or useful. Besides, these are often the product of a sober, thoughtful skepticism. They deserve more than epithets. So Heschel often makes no contact. Rather, he regularly offends men who do not have as firm a belief in God's revelation to the Jewish people as he has. And when they want to be believing Jews, when they are searching for some greater Jewish faith than that which they now have, to thrust them back so rudely with the left hand without seeking a way to draw them more closely to himself with the right seems to betray a faulty sympathy for their earnest if limited belief.

Such Jews, deeply concerned but uncommitted to the accuracy of the Biblical revelation or the binding authority of the rabbinic tradition, might be dismissed as self-seeking or self-hating were their argument only on the form of his presentation. They reject the Heschelian interpretation even as they reject other, older theories of verbal revelation on the substance of the case. That has nothing to do with vulgar reliance on Biblical science—if such an expression is still possible after generations of subjective imagination masquerading as objective expertise. Rather, it stems from the nature of the Biblical material itself which at its most compelling refutes the Godly authenticity of some of the rest. Thus Heschel, after his moving defense of the prophetic depiction of God's passability as accurate and acceptable, finally must deal with the descriptions of God's hot anger and violent wrath. What results is an insistence that this is never, like man's anger, out of moral control or surging from a depth which mixes with justice the demands of old hurts and ancient calls for vengeance. God's anger is always ethically constrained, argues Heschel. It is another form of God's justice which is passionately applied because men have done terrible deeds. One does not need to be a psychoanalyst to see the defensive posture here and the resulting rationalization. The harsh truth is that while God's justice may be difficult, his anger is a moral embarrassment. From what God has taught us about himself, men expect him to be righteous. However, anger is always unjust. It mixes with the deserved the undeserved, with this moment's deserts the effects of past events, with this person's guilt the evils done by others, real and imagined. God's anger is precisely not described by the prophets in terms of constraint or limitation. It is their exact point that now God is about to loose upon the Jews horrors greater than they could have anticipated for their acts and more than one would reasonably expect they deserve. The prophet uses the terror of God's anger as his last deterrent against their continuing sin. If one did not need to defend the accuracy of every major prophetic description concerning God, one could see some morality in the very human prophetic indignation at the people's continued obstinacy. Heschel must justify God's anger to preserve the prophetic reliability. So he is compelled to interpret away the clear-cut prophetic description of God's anger as unrestrained and therefore immoral.

The liberals were wrong in making too little of God and too much of man. Yet they knew that in all honesty to the text itself and to what else they knew about man and his history they could not accept the Biblical text and the rabbinic tradition as God-given or God-empowered. Slavery might be condoned by men in a given historical situation; it could never have been authorized by God. Women might be considered a separate and unequal category of humanity by societies up until recent times; any hint that this is God's permanent command must be repudiated. When these ideas and all of Judaism are integrated into what men have learned about the growth of ideas and practices, they become more believable if less authoritative than of old. Indeed, what now becomes a source of radical amazement is that though the Hebrews were so much a part of the civilization of the ancient Near East they yet managed to be so incredibly different; though the Jews have been intimately affected by all the major forces of human history they yet remained, creatively, a uniquely noble people.

One cannot help wondering if some of the problems connected with Heschel's theology are not more connected with his *aggadic,* nonlegal bent rather than his content. The rabbinic *aggada* is characterized not by structure but by partial truths, not by extended, harmonized reasoning but by moments of intense clarity. It abounds in contradiction and has no fear of imprecision or ambiguity. Classically, Jewish theology was in the *aggadic,* nonauthoritative mode. Heschel, whose English expositions seem almost a modern version of the old *aggadic* approach, may have revived its glories yet seems unable to eliminate its essential flaws. That, in significant part, is what makes the thought of Rabbi Joseph Baer Soloveitchik such an interesting complement to that of Abraham Joshua Heschel.

For nearly twenty-five years the theological fame of Rabbi Joseph B. Soloveitchik has had to rest, for those who have not known him personally, on the acclaim of his disciples, the eminent positions he holds, and, essentially, one long essay, *Ish Hahalachah* ("*Halachic* man"), published in 1944. Hints of his ideas on religion in general and of the development of Jewish law had from time to time been presented to the public, most notably by Emanuel Rackman and Aharon Lichtenstein. These intriguing glimpses of a major Jewish intellect aroused intense interest and anticipation in those who are concerned with contemporary Jewish thought, for Rabbi Soloveitchik, a master *halachist,* would seem uniquely qualified to undertake the task of Jewish theology. Most serious writers in the field have, by contrast, been distinguished by their competence in contemporary philosophy or theology. Their understanding of Judaism has been based largely on the *aggada,* the nonlegal rabbinic material, or medieval Jewish philosophy. Yet, as Franz Rosenzweig argued in his memorable essay on the proper methodology of Jewish theology, "Apologetisches Denken" ("Apologetic Thinking"), such efforts must remember that insofar as there was structure to Jewish religion over the centuries, it was provided by the halachah—and that was not mere speculation but the functioning norm of the autonomous Jewish community. Hence explicating the theology implied in the halachah has long been a goal of students of Jewish thought. Those, however, who could make their way through the swirling currents of the law seemed unable to chart its movements in terms of comprehensive religious concepts, while those who knew what might be an acceptable structure of modern thought often did not know "the small letters" in which the development of Jewish legal thinking must be traced. As head of the Rabbi Isaac Elchanan Theological Seminary of Yeshiva University and as chairman of the Halachah Commission of the Rabbinical Council of America, Rabbi Soloveitchik's authority to describe Judaism out of its legal tradition is beyond question. And his writing as well as his lectures over the years have demonstrated a continuing mastery of ancient and modern philosophical idiom, an ability already confirmed in 1931 by his doctorate, taken in the field of philosophy at the University of Berlin, with a dissertation on the thought of Hermann Cohen. Particularly since Soloveitchik has published so little, the recent appearance of several major essays by him has now made it possible for those who do not know him to take his thought into account.

Reading Rabbi Soloveitchik's work is a unique experience and a demanding one. Each of the major Jewish thinkers has a special style one must master before one can feel at home in his intellectual world. With Rabbi Soloveitchik as with Heschel, the style is critical to the effect of the thought. He writes with an individual sweep of intellect and passion of soul that makes his readers reach far beyond themselves. His ideas fly to the widest possible perspective, so that what seems a simple thought at the beginning of an essay soon leads on to the depths of the human soul or the heights of speculation about divinity. The unwary reader may easily lose the integrity of the argument in the broad span of its development. This outreach requires him to express himself in an exceedingly abstract way which in a less conscientious thinker might be an excuse for avoiding a confrontation with the philosophers who have previously traversed this path. Here Rabbi Soloveitchik's enormous erudition comes into play. There is continual, insightful reference to the history of human thought from Parmenides to contemporary theory of logic, from Catholic church fathers to modern playwrights. He does this purposefully and not in the fashion of those many writers who must impress by their intellectual name-dropping. The Jewish references run the gamut of the tradition, with the enlightening halachic interpretations the most rewarding of the many rich insights into the midrash, the liturgy, medieval philosophy, and mysticism. Often he crowns his conceptual structure with the interpretation of a familiar Biblical verse whose depth of meaning is now suddenly illuminated.

All this knowledge, however, is used to illustrate and amplify the ideas, not to demonstrate them. He is concerned neither to give an academic study of this historical development of a concept in Judaism nor to prove that this is the only consistent interpretation of the Jewish past. Rather, he presents his own ideas, here showing something of their foundation in Judaism, there revealing the nuances of his meaning by a comparison or contrast with a similar idea in the history of philosophy. He is thus more halachic than Baeck, more sophisticated than Kaplan, more erudite than Buber, more rationalistic than Heschel. Unfortunately, he has published so little that one cannot be certain one has a fair grasp of his general theological position, much less be able thoughtfully to evaluate it. Still, even the small sample of the work of so major a figure demands the attention of any serious student of Jewish theology.

Three major intellectual strands run through the available papers. The first of these is the acceptance of the dichotomy emphasized by Kant between the mathematical-scientific world, characterized by causality, and the inner life of man which, when it becomes fully human, is characterized by freedom and self-consciousness. Much of Rabbi Soloveitchik's writing is dialectical because of his acceptance of this division and he thus shuttles from the one level to the other, showing the contrast of the two and indicating the severe tensions that arise in man as a result of it. His appreciation of the reality of the scientifically described order of the universe seems to reach the level of metaphysical permanence so that, for example, he does not hesitate to label as allegory the references in the blessing over the new moon to the ultimate perfection of its "blemishes" (its changing size).

On the other hand, his treatment of the inner life of man is far from Kantian. That is not because he does not make frequent reference to the category of the ethical. He does, but it is by no means central to his discussion, nor is it altogether clear whether he would argue for the reality of an autonomous moral law for all rational beings. Rather, Rabbi Soloveitchik's understanding of the inner life of man comes within that broad stream of modern thought which is called existentialist. His emphasis is on the whole man and not just his mind. He is deeply concerned with the ambiguous and conflicted ontological situation in which man finds himself. His fundamental category for the discussion of religion in general is, apparently, loneliness. His mentors, though not his guides, in this direction, as he himself notes already in the 1944 essay, are Kierkegaard and Ibsen, but more especially, Scheler and Heidegger. (Since almost no one in the Jewish community in that period was concerned with such thinkers, it is not difficult to understand why his thought was little understood and drew only a small circle who might appreciate his ideas in depth as contrasted to giving him personal adulation. Yet despite the new openness to theology today in the Jewish community, one must be sobered by the recognition of the small number of Jews who are even now, two decades and more later, prepared cognitively to follow Rabbi Soloveitchik in his enterprise.)

These two threads are shaped and controlled by a third which assigns them their weight and value. All of Soloveitchik's writing apparently takes place within a fundamental structure of typology. He does not deal with things as they are, or even with abstractions from things as they are, but rather with pure possibilities of existence. These ideal forms are never found as such in the world, for all historic phenomena are necessarily imperfect manifestations of these ideal types and often the intersection of several of them. Nonetheless, the elucidation of such forms and their characteristics can help clarify the complexities of human existence. Rabbi Soloveitchik himself is quite explicit on his typological procedure, making specific reference to Eduard Spranger, whose various works popularized this type of thinking in Germany in the early twenties.

This typological foundation to his thought must be kept in mind as one reads the essays lest one think that they are dealing with historical reality and, as is typical in most philosophic or theological argument, an effort is being made to prove or demonstrate a truth. Thus an existentialist might argue from the reality of the human situation to the necessity for choice for or against God and thus seek by the force of the argument to move the reader to take a new stand. Because Rabbi Soloveitchik so often uses existentialist descriptions and because he so quickly moves from his pure types to the real situation of men, it would seem that something of that sort of argument is going on in his writings. Yet they do not try to lead or coerce the reader into a new choice or to insist that if he holds certain assumptions he ought to reach certain conclusions. He seems more concerned to explain than to convert. He is more involved in developed intellectual structures than is Heschel, but he too does not engage the reader in the latter's terms or explain his belief within the reader's universe of argument. He too speaks as a man of faith about his faith, staying well within its circle and not coming to its periphery to show the man standing there how, even perhaps why, he should make his way in. His typology then serves him as a hermeneutic device to elucidate the truth he knows. For one who believes that God has given the Torah and commanded man to search out its meaning, that would seem a most appropriate form for Jewish theological activity to take.

Rabbi Soloveitchik's thinking seems to rest on his analysis of man. In its fullest exposition to date he discerns a fundamental dualism in the nature of man which he elucidates through a typology of the two Adams in the creation stories. Adam the first is man the maker, controller, and user. Blessed by God with intelligence, he strives to conquer the earth and to use it for his good. In this effort he achieves the dignity which lifts him above the level of the brute and makes him man. He is thus naturally a social being, for community is useful in various work efforts and for the exchange which makes it possible for him to express his stature as a man of accomplishment. Though he can set moral norms for himself and experience great aesthetic creativity, these will not bring him ultimate satisfaction. He knows his limits, so that, even in the modern situation, he comes looking for God. The trouble is he insists on understanding God in his own manipulative terms. That is a contradiction which cannot be overcome and which sets up his conflict with Adam the second.

This pure type is of another orientation. He is submissive, accepting, for he knows himself to be the servant of God. He is less concerned with creating his own world than with taking the world as God has made it, for he sees God and hears his commandment in every aspect of it. In this intimate relationship with God he comes to know himself in all his uniqueness, for it is only in the fullness of his individual selfhood that he can come to know God. That knowledge, which gives him his true being, is therefore the most important reality of his life and yet it is inexpressible. It lies beyond all cognition or verbalization. So too, what it means for him to be a self is a matter of utter isolation, for he can never fully share it with anyone or communicate it to another. Yet God provides a place for him to ease his loneliness. It is the covenantal association in which God, "He," provides the link through which an "I" and a "Thou" can confront each other. This threesome is the model for every genuine community of faith, and only here does the man of faith find companionship and community, though never the overcoming of his ontic singleness.

A contrast with Martin Buber is helpful. Buber had said that while each individual maintains his ground in an encounter, the isolation is overcome. He is fully known by the other and indeed does not exist in his full individuality as a self outside the meeting. Rabbi Soloveitchik apparently takes a more atomistic, individualistic view of the self, though his dependence on Buber here is substantial.

Since Adam the first and Adam the second are typological structures which teach about men as they ideally are, it does not come as a surprise to hear that men, in fact, must live in both realms. The special problem of religion today is that Adam the first is so dominant culturally that only his way of thinking and speaking is given credence. He is interested in, even needful of, religion but insists that it be put in cognitive, controllable structures. Thus any man in whose soul Adam the second makes himself preeminent will feel an extra measure of loneliness in contemporary society. The truth on which he grounds his very existence is spurned and rejected. Adam the second is now driven back upon himself socially even as he always has been existentially, and thus he must live in two distinct dimensions of alienation.

A similar typological scheme provides the context of his discussion of the problem of evil. There he also speaks of man in two categories, the one a selfhood conferred by destiny which is contrasted to the selfhood which comes of relationship. The former type is characterized by the cognitive, speculative efforts of one who lives in the world of cause and effect and whose search for a theodicy must end in despair since he insists on rational solutions. The second type, however, breaks through the natural order to become a free, creative subject, a partner of God in the work of creation. Loving God, he does not ask metaphysical questions. He accepts what comes as God's task for his welfare and instead inquires what he is now required to do. Man is necessarily of both types. As the former he can never be satisfied with theologies of suffering and must continually seek new ones. As a man of faith he lives content with God and unconcerned about answers.

In connection with his discussion of Christian-Jewish theological dialogue he speaks of man on three separate and progressive levels of being, again basing himself on the Biblical account of creation. The first level is natural and hedonic, with man so much at home in the universe that he does not even see it as task or opportunity. On the second level, man is confronted by nature and reaches out to tame it with his cognitive and normative talents. On the third level, he is the one who confronts other persons, and in so doing, realizes that though he may find the joys of companionship, he will never be able to overcome the barrier that separates his true self from the other. In this typology, a new level of being, the first, has been introduced into the scheme, and since the author specifically states that he is speaking of man in modern times when he uses this description it would be of great interest to know the relation of this natural man to the scheme of the two Adams. Again, the third level seems somewhat different from that of Adam the second. Most probably these questions are a result of the paucity of the materials available, which does not permit of even this small effort at systematization.

The social forms of human existence are discussed by Rabbi

Soloveitchik in terms of these characterizations of the individual. Thus though Adam the second makes possible covenantal associations, one cannot simply identify a given historic religious community with a real community of faith. Religion as an institution necessarily mixes the various ideal modes of human existence, the natural and the covenantal. To expect that joining or participating in a given institution of religion will necessarily bring one into the sort of covenant existence which assuages existential loneliness is folly. The same sort of analysis is used to describe the people of Israel, going so far as to describe God as having made two distinct covenants with Israel, one in Egypt and another at Sinai. Utilizing corporately now the terminology for individuals, he calls them, respectively, a covenant of destiny and a covenant of relationship. The former describes Jewishness in the sense of the situation into which a Jew is born, a common past, a common suffering, a common responsibility. The latter is a matter of choice, the Jewish religious task which the community may seek to ignore or freely to fulfill. And while the special Jewish experience may not be the best measure by which to judge Rabbi Soloveitchik's attitude toward all social groups or religions, this Jewish analysis is sufficiently like the difference between the associations formed by Adam the first and Adam the second that this particular illustration of his general social theory seems reliable.

True communities of faith may best be distinguished from one another (though theoretically not evaluated) in terms of the individuals they seek to create. Thus Rabbi Soloveitchik takes great care to distinguish the halachic approach to holiness from that found in more subjective types of religion and halachic man from religious man in general. In some religions the sphere of the holy is a means of withdrawal from life. Religion is the sanctuary of escape from problems and difficulties. Rabbi Soloveitchik, cognizant of the full existential torment of man torn between the two Adams within him, will not accept peace of mind as the goal of religion. Halachic man does have a sense of certainty and assurance but it does not come from a magical resolution of his ontological problems or a flight from them. Rather, it is the result of confronting all that life has to offer, recognizing amidst the turmoil that every trial comes from God and that he can be served in truth as one moves forward in obedient acceptance. For the distinctive characteristic of the halachah is that it takes what might have been a purely subjective and personal faith and channels it into specific times and places, thereby rooting man in the real world in all its fullness. In so doing, it resolves the inner conflict of the two Adams. Its specification requires that Adam the second turn his intimately felt relationship into deeds in the objective order of existence; yet at the same time as Adam the first is about to be happy with an objective religious realm he can use to aggrandize himself, the halachah continually reminds him that his service is to God.

Here one cannot help seeing a careful effort to dissociate this thinking from the various forms of Protestant existentialism, particularly those somewhat vulgar varieties which sought to blend Kierkegaard's austere concern with self with romantic reliance upon experience derived from Schleiermacher and Otto. Much of this attack on the religious as such seems an implicit polemic against Christianity, if, as is easy, one takes religious man as the Christian par excellence and halachic man as the Jew. Yet that easy identification will not do, not only because Rabbi Soloveitchik indicates again and again that he is speaking of pure types but also because it is clear that there are other types of Jew than halachic man. While Rabbi Soloveitchik contrasts the latter very favorably with mystic man, using many citations from the literature of Chabad Hasidism to illustrate that type, he does not say that Jewish mystics are not somehow Jews, even good Jews, though he obviously believes halachic man is a superior type of Jew. Indeed, the essay *Ish Hahalachah* is a *mitnaged,* anti-Hasidic phenomenology of awesome proportions.

The problem involved here, the precise application or significance of a typology, inheres in the choices of this intellectual tool. Typologies may be illuminating but it is never clear whence the types arise; why these and not others are selected; how the various types used for various situations relate to one another; what gives the total universe of types its integrity. Thus, a Christian might well argue, if the *ish hahalachah* is a pure type—and if he is a particularly Jewish type, why do Jews have separate pure forms?—must the *ish hahalachah* necessarily be a Jew? It is clear that Protestant Christians would rarely fall under such a typology, but almost all the characteristics mentioned of halachic man could easily be applied to personality types well known in Roman Catholicism, particularly in the Jesuit order. Such a methodologically proper universalization of the types would almost certainly change the way in which most Jews unconsciously read Rabbi Soloveitchik, though he is not to blame for their unconscious conversion of his typologies into value judgments or an authorization for Jewish practices.

Another example of the problem of working with typologies may help clarify some of the difficulties inherent in this method. Rabbi Soloveitchik uses his one tripartite analysis of man, referred to above, to argue that while Jews share in the common cultural and social welfare activities of men on level two, the progress to level three brings men to faith and utter individuality. While men in this mode may join in association with other men of similar faith, their basic sense of certainty remains ultimately incommunicable. From this pure, typological truth the inference is then drawn on the realistic level that Jews and Christians, even under conditions of complete equality, even to learn what constitutes their differences and uniqueness, should not seek to discuss theology with one another.

What is the methodological basis for such unqualified extrapolation from the realm of ideal types to the real human situation? To be sure, men do have incredible difficulty in communicating with one another, yet Rabbi Soloveitchik's own efforts to clarify the nature of the life of faith on a universal human, as well as a specifically Jewish, level belie, by their very success, the theoretical futility of such efforts—at least as far as real human beings and not pure types of humanity are involved. For though men cannot know all or as much as they would like to know about another man's faith, they must be able to know something significant about it, or else they could not know whether they themselves are in the right community of faith or when they might admit a convert to their faith. One might rather equally well argue that even as a contrast with the communicating other only confirms men in their loneliness, so theological discussions with other faith communities carried out in full self-respecting emphasis on differences should strengthen one's sense of Jewish uniqueness while helping Jews understand better, in their distance, the men and institutions with whom they must face a dangerous history.

If the major problem of going beyond existentialist Jewish theologies is their inability to ground structures of Jewish action, then it is difficult to see how a typological theology can be of any greater help. In existentialist interpretations, at least, an understanding is provided of the individual's sense of authority in a given situation. Deductions to reality from pure types are never valid. Knowing them does not say anything about what a real man must do in the real world. The reason Rabbi Soloveitchik can be content with a typological framework to his thought is that he does not need theological reasoning to authorize action. That matter is already settled in his faith in divine revelation of both the written and the oral law. He can know, though, this is neither as simple nor as free of anxiety as it often seems to the nonorthodox, what God wants him to do. His theology follows upon that reality. It does not presume to substantiate it. Rather, it seeks to illumine the meaning of such believing existence particularly, in the writings to date, in its universal aspect. This is, thus far, more a Jewish theology of religion in general than a form of general theologizing which seeks to explain the uniqueness and particularity of Judaism. The virtue of the typologizing is that it brings a cognitive pattern into the man of faith's discussion of what he knows but equally knows cannot properly be expressed. Where Heschel uses his style, shock, and his inversion of the questions to awaken and evoke, Soloveitchik utilizes a directly intellectual device and is therefore far more helpful to the average thoughtful but uncommitted inquirer. Even though his types and their interaction remain pure ideals, still in their architectural integrity and in their continual relevance to the concrete situations in which men find themselves, they are quite compelling. For a moment the life of faith as seen by faith stands open.

Yet what remains missing is the way by which modern man might come to such faith. In his secularity what he finds most difficult to accept, what his sense of autonomy and the lessons of history as he sees it will not let him accept, is the traditional Jewish doctrine of revelation. That may be axiomatic to Heschel and Rabbi Soloveitchik, but that is where the modern Jewish inquirer needs his greatest help. The traditionalist theologian needs either to establish its reality for him or more reasonably to help him find a way to believe in it. Heschel does speak to that subject. Soloveitchik thus far does not. From what has been said above, it would seem reasonable to conclude that he cannot. His typological method, particularly in its reliance on existentialist categories, is almost certainly incapable of that task. Rather, he uses the theology to argue that the fundamental faith is ineffable. It substantiates the limiting of the discussable. That is both its strength and its defect, for most Jews do not share that faith today. If, inquiring about a belief he might like to hold but finds he cannot, a Jew hears it is beyond analysis and argument, then this theology is not for him. The question then is one of audience or, at least, of approach. How much can one assume and still maintain a community of meaning? How much can one question and still remain true to one's faith or one's tradition of belief?

Because these questions divide those who accept as fundamental the classic understanding of the Sinaitic revelation from those who do not, there must be two basic types of Jewish theology today, orthodox and liberal. The division is common in several faiths today and even from this brief discussion, it is clear why two forms of theologizing tend to arise. For the neoliberal it remains clear that, despite the effort to overcome the failings of the older liberalism, he cannot return to orthodoxy whether in the form of Heschel's mitigated fundamentalism or whether that made relevant by the existentialist-oriented typologies of Rabbi Soloveitchik. They believe too much, so they explain too little. They may still serve as personal models of faith linked to modernity. Their theological methods cannot serve the needs of those who would speak to Jews of some but not as encompassing a faith. That is not to say that what is needed is theology for the cynical or the embittered, the superior or the disdainful, for without some personal conversion religious discussion with them is probably impossible. That is not what is being sought. There are many seriously questioning men who yet know themselves to be and to believe as Jews. How can the space between Judaism, taken more seriously than in the liberal past, yet not in full tradition, and the current age, yet not accepted with its full disbelief, be bridged? How does postmodern Judaism speak to postmodern man? That old question of emancipated Jewry, now freshly put, remains central.

Part Three

IN SEARCH OF A STANCE

8

BETWEEN LIBERALISM AND THE NEW ORTHODOXY

FAITH may have three separate though related levels of meaning in modern Jewish theology. It may connote commitment to action, commitment to content, and mostly, commitment to a basic premise. Each level of significance has its particular implications for theological method and must therefore be treated on its own.

On the first level, to say that Jewish theology involves faith means, at least, that the Jewish theologian is expected to live what he teaches. Of the philosopher of religion one can demand only that he understand the reasoning of religious thinkers, not that he believe and live by all the diverse systems he expounds. A theologian should be no less academically competent and proficient, but in his case one critical requirement is added which radically changes the context of his scholarship. He shares the faith he expounds, and so his life should show his strength of belief in the truths he proclaims.

If faith today must include both acts and thoughts, it is because of frequent experience with those whose concepts are persuasive but whose behavior is repulsive. Not all men who think bright thoughts, not even those who are persuaded of their truth, actually live by them, even most of the time. This gap between cognition and decision, between idea and resolve, cannot be ignored. We may not ourselves believe much, but we will judge the man who says he believes, more by his performance than by his preaching.

In Judaism, in which action has traditionally been valued above thought, the theologian's life must be the first evidence of his teaching. And for a Jew, that must inevitably mean not just his private and familial existence but his participation in the ongoing activity of the synagogue and the Jewish people as a whole. Those rabbis who attended the Hebrew Union College in Cincinnati in the forties as I did saw Samuel Cohon's vast Jewish learning in the classroom, but when we spent a Sabbath evening in his home, then we had a touch of Samuel Cohon the Jew, and in his living saw his theology fulfilled. No wonder, despite the Pauline associations he vigorously opposed, he suggested as a verse for one of the then-new stained-glass windows in the college chapel Habakkuk's proclamation: "The righteous shall live by his faith."

At this level there is virtual unanimity among Jews. The Jewish theologian should live his understanding of Judaism, and through his Jewish living he should test and refine his Judaism. But Jewish action stems from an understanding of the content of Judaism, and that content is itself established through faith. Surprising as it may seem, that is the almost unanimous conclusion of contemporary Jewish thinkers. Take, for example, the absolutely central question: How do we know there is a God? Even those Jewish theologians who are committed to the utmost use of reason acknowledge that at a given point reason will carry them no farther. It may prepare the way. It may be necessary for clarification afterward, but reason itself does not lead them to the conclusion that there really is a God. The only way to get to Judaism's position is by faith.

Mordecai Kaplan has said: Belief in God "is an assumption that is not susceptible of proof"[1] and "Whence do we derive this faith in a Power that endorses what ought to be? Not from that aspect of the mind which has to do only with mathematically and logically demonstrated knowledge. Such faith stems from that aspect of the mind which finds expression in the enthusiasm for living, in the passion to surmount limitations."[2] Elsewhere he speaks of it as an intuition or an affirmation of one's whole being.[3]

Levi Olan similarly acknowledges that "the God of faith is not subject to proof in the rational or scientific sense. . . . Ultimately, as Judaism learned at the beginning, God is an affirmation and a postulate."[4] What affirmations and postulates involve is made clear by him in another connection: Faith by its very nature involves affirmations *beyond the rational* [italics mine, E.B.B.] and the Hebraic spirit is not characterized by a rigid syllogistic encasement."[5] Similarly, Roland Gittelsohn, in the course of his argument for the existence of God, says: "The mind . . . by itself, unaided by the heart, . . . can never provide total answers. . . . We need faith. Man cannot live by reason alone. . . . Of course we need faith to carry us beyond the bounds of reason."[6]

Liberal Jews are so accustomed to hearing these men called "rationalists" that they tend to accept that appellation naïvely. They begin to believe that such thinkers are true philosophic rationalists, that if they follow their views, they may hope to dispense with the kind of faith which the thinkers categorize as "beyond the rational" or "beyond the bounds of reason." But the unreflective have only themselves to blame for this illusion. The thinkers themselves have been far more rigorous and honest. They say plainly, "Men need faith." Their claim to the title "rationalist" does not derive from their elimination of faith but from their effort to control faith by reason, as discussed below.

There have been Jewish thinkers in ages past, not only in medieval times, but as recently as Hermann Cohen, who were thoroughgoing philosophic rationalists. These men sought to demonstrate the truth about the existence of God out of a rigorously intellectual argument. In this, the simple philosophic meaning of the term, it would be true to say, there are no rationalists among liberal Jewish theologians today.

This description is not limited to naturalists. Leo Baeck, often considered a "rationalist" by the uncritical, is rather to be found with those who clearly confess reason's inadequacy to establish a Jewish view of God. One might have expected Baeck, as a faithful though independent follower of Hermann Cohen, to restate Cohen's philosophical demonstration of the necessity of the idea of God. Baeck completely avoids this and instead, following Schleiermacher, bases his discussion on inner experience, grounds that would have been repugnant to the Marburg Neo-Kantian. Thus it is not God as idea, but God as Exalted One, as Mystery, as Secret, that Baeck often speaks of him. Moreover, Baeck does not wait for the end of a long rationally ordered argument to introduce faith as the means of reaching a triumphant conclusion. God in all his shroudedness as well as his righteousness is present from the very beginning of Baeck's discussion. When in his chapter on "Faith in God" he discusses faith directly, he says:

> In Judaism faith is nothing but the living consciousness of the Omnipresent. . . . This conviction is not sustained by speculation and gnosis, or by facts and proofs. Hence there is in it nothing subtly reasoned out, nothing demonstrated or expounded. On the contrary, it is the opposite of the faith which has to be set forth by arguments or established by victories.[7]

Only Martin Buber, among contemporary thinkers, finds God by knowledge, so to speak, rather than by faith. Buber manages this by an epistemology which has two categories of knowing, object-knowing and subject-knowing. The latter is as natural and everyday as the former. It involves no special state of consciousness and is clearly not to be compared with the mystic's special experience. Buber says men know God as they know other subjects, save that he is noncorporeal. Thus faith for Buber is not a way of reaching convictions about God, but the life which comes from knowing him.

Philosophically, one cannot insist a priori that it is impossible that knowledge is available in two modes each with its appropriate structure and value. If Buber's categories are right, it would seem just as rational to know subjects by subject-knowing as it is to know objects objectively. In those terms one might facetiously suggest that Buber is the only "rationalist" among Jewish philosophers today. But the title has now lost all meaning. Though faith has become knowing for Buber, what he has really shown is that all subjects are known by faith, and that faith is more common to life than most modern men had thought.

Thus, there is almost universal agreement among contemporary writers that faith is basic to Jewish theology, not only on the level of action, but on the more fundamental level of content as well.[8]

Once faith has been admitted to Jewish theology, a third and deeper plane of discussion arises. Faith conduces to such fundamental Jewish affirmations as the existence of God, his goodness, and its eventual triumph. But what else will it bring? Are modern Jews prepared to accept everything that has been characteristic of believing Jews over the centuries? Admitting faith to religiosity raises the danger of Orthodoxy and sets the liberal Jew in search of a principle by which to regulate the content faith may contribute to his liberal Judaism.

The need for a regulative principle is prompted too by a knowledge of human history. Summoning the deepest of men's passions, faith may lead to superstition, fanaticism, and oppression, and it has done so among Jews as among other peoples. Perhaps a liberal Jew could somehow reconcile Orthodox Jewish observance with his liberalism, if his personal decision so demanded. But that his faith might bring him into conflict with his sense of morality is as intolerable as it is a realistic possibility. For this reason, even more than because of Orthodoxy, a means of controlling faith must be found.

In traditional Judaism the search would quickly be over. The halachic tradition of authentic interpretation would do this in theory, even as the sanctions of the observant, organized

Jewish community would do so in practice. But for liberal Jews, who have neither a unifying law nor an observant community to channel their faith, but who rather require a firm faith so that they may rally the community and reestablish standards of Jewish living, the regulating principle must be found on the personal, not the communal level.

How has this need been met over the past one hundred or so years of liberal Jewish theology? For Geiger, the progress that history displayed in its systematic evolution was the criterion of his Jewish faith. In its name he could abandon the personal Messiah. For Leo Baeck, God's will is always understood as an ethical demand, and ethical monotheism is the test of Judaism. For this reason he makes the Jewish people a means to preserve and foster ethical monotheism, and Jewish observance a secondary means to preserve that primary means. With Buber, though faith is a kind of knowing, one is commanded only as one encounters or is personally encountered. Thus Buber is halachically more radical than the most radical Reform Jew and rejects any practice that stems from community tradition rather than personal experience.

For Mordecai Kaplan, the modern, naturalistic, particularly social scientific understanding of man and society are indispensable. This, he believes, requires him to posit an impersonal God. Roland Gittelsohn's argument carries this view of reason as the arbiter of faith to its fullest and clearest exposition. Now come the sentences that follow the previous citation and thus give his thought his own completion:

> Of course we need faith to carry us beyond the bounds of reason. But that faith must be built on a foundation of reason, must be consistent with the reasonable and the known, not contradictory to them. If the direction of the knowledge yielded by experience and reason be represented by a solid line, faith must be a dotted line which continues in the same general direction, not one which goes off at a capricious and contradictory angle.[9]

Here faith is strictly bound by reason, and Gittelsohn's reason can permit him to have faith in only a limited God.

One may, with some hesitation, summarize this cursory survey. Liberal Jewish thinkers have generally sought to regulate their faith by finding a universal standard of truth and reinterpreting Judaism in its terms. This standard has usually been borrowed from the philosophy current in the theologian's time and place, though Cohen and Buber created their own. If liberal Jewish thinkers, excepting Cohen, deserve to be called rationalists, though they rely on faith and cannot dispense with it, it is because they have regularly sought to control their faith by some rational principle.

What principle is most appropriate today?

Before a reply is offered to this question, the responsibility involved in making that decision should be made abundantly clear. The choice of a principle to guide the operation of faith is not a modest technical matter. It involves the very heart of Judaism. Selecting one concept pattern over another is already committing oneself to a certain character in his Judaism, not just its beliefs, but the balance and weight of its observances as well. This principle changes the nature of God, alters Israel's character, and reforms the hierarchy of Jewish values, as seen above. This is the most fundamental decision man can make with regard to his religion.

For some men the response is relatively easy. They recognize in one or another contemporary philosophic system man's best guide to truth, and they interpret Judaism through it. But for most men the choice is not that simple, particularly when they look at the views which previous thinkers have espoused.

If they turn to the vaguely Hegelian trust in historic progress of either a Geiger or a Kohler, they find themselves in most uncongenial territory. History is not always progressive, and it is difficult to say with conviction that thinkers today know the truth of man and God better and more clearly than did a previous age. It is clear, however, that one cannot, as they did, unselfconsciously choose what one wishes in history and by calling it "the highest," "the noblest," or "the best," consider it validated by the historical march of truth.

The rational idealism of Cohen, even as modified by Baeck, is similarly problematic. In the former case, what is its relation to the real world? How can one make the transfer from the philosophically necessary idea to the concretely existing reality? And in both cases, how can a thinker today reestablish a philosophic certainty which derives from the clarity and independence of the ethical demand? Liberal Jews obviously do not wish to compromise the significance or the authority of the ethical. But it is another thing to make ethics the one sure and self-substantiating foundation of all other affirmations of value. The varying apprehensions of ethical responsibility among different peoples, and even in different social classes within Western society itself, as well as the role education and personal exposure play in determining conscience, all make of the ethical a problem to be dealt with, rather than an unshakable base on which to build.

Nor is the scientific naturalism of Kaplan, Olan, and Gittelsohn any less troublesome. Perhaps in the thirties it was possible to hold simply and self-evidently, as Kaplan did, that to be modern necessarily meant to think in terms of naturalism.[10] Today there are clearly other ways of being sophisticatedly modern, particularly since naturalism has floundered in dealing with the key philosophic problem of our time, the identification and authorization of values. One can take a thoroughgoing scientific view of reality and come up a moral neutral, as the atomic bomb so dramatically illustrated. Such an uncommitted naturalism is far more rationalistic, that is, internally consistent, than is Kaplan's theism. His response to this charge is that such a naturalism cannot motivate morality, and therefore must be rejected.[11] Philosophically, if the morality is prior, Kaplan should, like the Neo-Kantians, first rationally establish the realm of the ethical, which he never does. Practically, it is simply not true that naturalists, agnostic philosophically in regard to God or ethics, cannot be morally active, as the cases of Bertrand Russell and others make clear.

Gittelsohn's more tightly drawn argument from science suffers from a similar difficulty. If scientific reason knows anything, it is that superfluous hypotheses are rigorously to be excluded. To add God to a strictly scientific view of the universe is therefore not to continue in a direction previously established but to add a new and rationally unnecessary direction. It is not just adding a bit of spice to the food stuff, but radically changing the menu.

Of course, if what Gittelsohn means is that God seems a "reasonable" addition to the scientific view of the universe, that is another matter. It is a far cry from the philosophically ordered "rational" to what one personally can believe, the "reasonable." What makes the addition of God so reasonable to Gittelsohn is that he already believed in him before the argument began. Indeed, it would be difficult to explain why Gittelsohn prefers the scientific data and opinions which will make the addition of God reasonable to all that which would not, if it were not that he begins with faith in God. Thus while Gittelsohn claims that faith only completes a line which rationality itself drew, it seems clear that faith here preceded reason and guided it.

Levi Olan, who has given a similar argument about man's place in the universe, has been far more precise on the matter of presuppositions. While insisting that reason is a fundamental ingredient of truth, in his discussion of faith and reason he has frankly noted, "Reason, of itself is never the source of truth."[12] Thus he correctly calls his evidence from modern science neither proofs nor even indications but resources. In other words, having established by faith that he believes in man, he can then find much substantiation in modern science for such a view.

These previous choices—historic progress, idealism, naturalism—do not easily commend themselves today as a means of guiding faith. Perhaps then one should turn to the current fashions in philosophy: linguistic analysis, Tillichian ontology, or one of the varieties of religious (not atheistic!) existentialism. Perhaps, dissatisfied with all the alternatives, one ought instead to begin by creating one's own system of universal truth.

Which of these living if troublesome options should be chosen?

But considering what is at stake, one should first ask, "*How* choose?" On what basis shall one decide whether to adopt one principle or another to regulate his faith? This question may with equal significance be asked of the man who is not troubled by such uncertainty but knows which philosophy he must follow. How does he know it? How did he determine it?

Three possibilities suggest themselves. At one time it might have been possible to suggest that certain truths were self-evident, or so clear and distinct that one could not doubt them. Obviously a philosophy that based itself on them was sound. Such a view could be accepted by only a few today. Modern men have learned to doubt everything, not the least themselves, their certainty, and their intuitions. To be modern is, to begin with, to be critical.

Perhaps, then, one should see his choice more as a hypothesis, an educated guess, a temporary venture whose validity will be determined as he experiences the results of its use and its application to life.

In many ways that is an attractive suggestion. Surely, few consider themselves to be in possession of absolute truth here and now. Liberals particularly do not want to take up a dogmatic stand, one that is not open to change and the possibility of whose further refinement is rejected in advance.

But with all the determination to remain open to new and keener truth, it is difficult indeed to call the principle sought a tentative surmise. Consider what is involved in this decision. On this "hypothesis" the whole of religion hangs. What is at stake is simply—*everything*. A commitment of such intense involvement and immense consequence is not merely an enlightened hunch about what might possibly turn out to be right. In all its momentariness, in all its openness to readjustment, it cannot be called less than an act of faith.

Indeed, the very structure of the decision itself makes that clear. When one judges among alternate possibilities of reason (in fact, when one stands before any single system of reason asking whether he shall use it), he cannot use reason itself as the basis of decision. The criterion of the adequacy of reason cannot be reason itself, for it is precisely reason that is being judged. Or, to put the matter more directly, every philosophy begins with an act of faith. That is what is meant by saying each person inevitably has his own assumptions. Assumptions are not validated by reason. They are an expression of faith.

On this point, too, Olan has been far more clear and consistent than other rationalists. Beginning in 1947 (as far back as I have been able to trace the matter), he has openly referred to liberalism as a "faith." His essay in the collection *Reform Judaism* is appropriately entitled "Rethinking the Liberal Faith."[13] And his address to the Central Conference of American Rabbis in 1963 was on the theme "New Resources for a Liberal Faith."[14] Olan does not seek to prove the rational necessity of liberalism. Rather, he admits that liberalism is a faith, one that is consistent with reason but clearly not established by it. Faith establishes the matrix, and then, within its frame, reason is fully free to operate.

In short, in choosing a regulative principle one confronts a paradox. One does not arrive at the content of Judaism without faith, but liberals also believe they cannot affirm everything to which believing Jews in the past few centuries have been committed. That is why they seek to limit their faith in Judaism by some sort of regulating principle. Only now it is clear that no self-justifying, autonomous principle exists, but all the possibilities themselves involve a prior act of faith.

Thus, one can delimit Jewish faith only by acknowledging that one has a prior faith in whose name he is willing to alter and revise traditional Judaism. This is the third and deepest level of faith on which the Jewish theologian must take a stand, commitment not only to action or to content, but to one particular beginning. Thus the structure of Jewish theology is tripartite and its work is dialectical. It begins in faith and this makes possible the work of reason which, in turn, ends with faith—from this point on, it is always faith followed by reason followed by faith in infinite, better messianic development.

So the question remains, In which approach shall liberals today put their faith?

From this point on I should not speak of what liberals should choose. Rather, in accord with what I said on the first level about the theologian's thought and life, I must speak of what I find I must choose and the method that derives from it. I hope that there are others who share my commitments and that I am articulating their view, consciously held or not, as well as my own.

My position is simple: I believe the general method of Jewish theology over these past hundred years no longer makes sense. It reflects a point of view that may once have been necessary or even desirable, but is so no longer. And it is time consciously to confront this issue and radically alter course.

Perhaps I can clarify my position by a question, hypothetical, to be sure, but not unrealistic. Suppose I follow the traditional method of liberal Jewish theology and choose an intellectual medium for my faith, say Neo-Kantianism, existentialism, or modern secularity. I carefully work out the meaning of Judaism in its terms, adding some insights on the one hand, but also refusing to believe this or observe that, on the other. Whereupon, over the years, I discover that the philosophy in which I had placed such faith is not nearly as adequate to life as I thought. Indeed, I now wish to replace it with a better one. But wait. I had based my Judaism on that philosophy. In its name I had both justified and revised my Judaism. Once I have lost faith in the philosophy, do I lose faith in Judaism as well? Would I in the face of this intellectual setback conclude that Judaism itself no longer has meaning for me?

Some men have indeed given up their Judaism under such circumstances, but I would like to believe that I would not, and the majority of Jews would not either. Despite such an intellectual catastrophe I would insist that I know Judaism is still true. And I would do so despite the crash of reason and the tragedy of this experience, because my belief in Judaism was deeper than my trust in any philosophy.

Theologians in the past century have acted as if they knew a truth superior to Judaism. But I do not know a body of knowledge or a system of understanding God and man and history superior to Judaism. I do not have a faith more basic to my existence than my Judaism. I believe in Judaism, not because there are such good expositions of its content and its meaning, but despite all the inadequate and clumsy statements of its substance, including my own. I should be delighted one day to have a philosophically tenable exposition of the truth of Judaism, but I shall not wait for one to believe in it. My faith in Judaism comes before any other faith I have, and I want to make this priority of faith in Judaism my methodological starting point.

What is of critical concern to me is the level on which Jews make their commitment to Judaism. Two examples from congregational life should clarify the implications of this ranking.

Most theologians have had to deal with intellectuals whose approach to life was genuinely framed in terms of a given mental pattern. When such a man inquires seriously about Judaism, we are eager to tell him of its truth but usually have great difficulty in doing so. The reason is clear. This man has a prior faith. The only way one can make oneself understood, and, hopefully, convincing to him, is to translate Judaism into the terms of his prior faith. And that is just the trouble. Often his private faith is so constructed that it does not make possible a belief in God, or, to him worse, an institutionalized religion. But whether he already has a hospitable or inhospitable point of view, one must recognize its priority in his life and talk to him in his terms. That is why it is so difficult to do so satisfactorily.

This task of explaining one's faith to a man with another faith has an old and honorable theological history. Its name is unfortunate. It is called apologetics. Much of the theologian's work not only with intellectuals but with synagogue Jews is apologetic theology. And, in general, liberal Jewish theology this past century has been essentially apologetic. Perhaps unconsciously it seems to have assumed that it was addressing nonbelievers. It then took up its argument in terms the nonbeliever could hopefully accept and sought to explain Judaism convincingly in them.

Apologetics is an important practical task, not only for the Jew who does not believe but also for all those men of goodwill who seek Judaism's truth. The believer has a responsibility to share such truth as he has found. But apologetics cannot be the theologian's primary intellectual task today. Before he devises a theology for the outsider, he must clarify what those inside the circle of faith share.

If faith in Judaism is prior to any other body of truth, then it is entitled to receive intellectual attention in its own right, not just as explanation in terms of another point of view.

More critical to this issue of priority is the case of those who have some faith in Judaism. Why does their Judaism generally have so little impact on their lives? Why is it so often so difficult to communicate to them the overwhelming importance of Jewish belief and observance? Here too the answer may be found in analyzing the level of their Jewish faith. They do believe in Judaism but they have other faiths of greater importance. As long as Judaism can be explained in terms of their private world of belief, they will accept it. One can win their willingness to Jewish action when it is explained in their terms, say mental health or the image of themselves as good parents, dutiful children, or loyal Americans. But let the demands transgress their private norms, say a call for mid-week Hebrew study, daily prayer, or public agreement to racially integrated housing, and Judaism has become parochial, pietistic, political.

That is the danger of marketing Judaism in the consumer's terms, of always doing apologetics. One covertly endorses the private faith by which the inquirer lives rather than shaking him loose from his more basic belief. Judaism never becomes the foundation of his life, so he uses it when it suits his purposes and rejects it when it does not.

Many people are attracted to Reform Judaism for just this reason, not because it is "convenient," but because they know Reform stands committed to freedom of individual conscience. It will not deny each man's right to spiritual self-determination. The result in many cases has been that many liberal Jews seem to believe first in themselves, their needs, their goals, their image, and only on a secondary level in Judaism, its God, its commandments, its aspirations. And that is why every sensitive servant of the God of Israel suffers so as he works with his people. A religion that takes second place is no religion. Unless Judaism is fully primary in the lives of Jews, that first step has been neglected on which all the rest of the journey depends.

Liberal Judaism is committed both to the self and to the tradition. Previous generations sought regularly to put the self first, to work from the self back to the tradition. In part they were right. The individual must always be the foundation of belief and thus retain the right to disbelieve. Respect for his freedom makes the right of dissent inalienable.

The problem then becomes: How can one give primary allegiance to a tradition he cannot accept as absolute? Can one retain the self's right to judge and to dissent, without turning it into a rival principle of faith? That is indeed what I am suggesting. By faith in Judaism I mean the conscious, personal assent to the unique meaningfulness and significance of the Jewish religious tradition for our lives. Such faith affirms a qualitative distinction between the truth given us about God, man, and history in Judaism and in any other system or structure, without thereby insisting that Judaism is always right or cannot learn much from other sources. Being founded on individual assent, it likewise guarantees the right to dissent without thereby raising the self to the status of a prior principle.

The faith by which I seek to live as a liberal Jew is therefore a vigorous affirmation of the primacy of Judaism for my life if not of its absolute character. If I am consistently and rigorously to carry on the work of theology in its terms, a fourfold process suggests itself.

First, it should be obvious that such Jewish theology begins not with an idealist, naturalist, ontological, or linguistic philosophy, or an existential diagnosis of the self, but with the tradition and its affirmation. Nor will the disciplined detachment of a Buchler or a Marmorstein, or the quiet appreciation of a Schechter or a Moore, suffice. They saw the Jewish past as an object of investigation. I see it rather as having a claim upon me and my life reasonably similar to that which it had upon other generations of Jews. Their careful objectivity can only be a beginning for a search which now must also ask: What did it mean once to believe such a faith? What did it mean to try to live such a faith? And, most important, what does it mean for me to join my forefathers in this belief? I begin with the tradition not as an interesting curio from the past or a source of quotations to illustrate some modern view, but as a living content of belief which confronts me in authority and challenge.

Nor can I, in the second place, say in advance that I should limit my attention and concern to just those aspects which are relevant. Because I assert no principle prior to Judaism, I cannot know beforehand what no longer has the power to speak to me and to guide my life. I must pay as much attention to the priesthood as to the prophets, to the rabbinic apocalypses and mysticisms as to their ethics. And I must, if I would be true to this faith, remain as open as possible to what Jewish tradition can teach, even if that means I might end up believing it all. The methodological principle here is to seek to make faith in Judaism self-regulating. Once prophecy was that judgment from within which helped the tradition transcend itself. My hope is that an open confrontation with Jewish faith can show the way to an ever truer Judaism.

Third, my openhearted search of the tradition may from time to time lead me to dissent. Because I do not wish to make a faith of dissent, I hope not to search to disagree nor study to disavow. In my affirmation of the primary value of Judaism I cannot easily or peacefully dissociate myself from its teachings. When in all seriousness I am moved to disagree, the responsibility now rests upon me to justify that disagreement. Previous generations of liberal Jews often acted as if Judaism had to justify itself to the Jew. I am arguing that making Jewish faith primary calls on me to justify myself when I dissent from it.

Nor do I worry that this shift of responsibility will make it difficult for the liberal to remain free and selective. One can rely not only on his decades of autonomy and the influence of the American environment to strengthen his will to think for himself but on the instinctive human disinclination to accept duty and responsibility freely.

This affirmation of the right to dissent is the reason I cannot follow the theological methodology of Abraham Heschel. Omitting now all questions of the literary form in which he puts his arguments, the content does seek to be true to the Jewish tradition in its own terms. While he is no simple fundamentalist and makes allowances for the humanity of revelation, he does not understand genuine dissent. Again and again he asks whether it is believable that a Biblical author should lie or misrepresent. Again and again he characterizes possible alternative thoughts as unthinkable or unbelievable.[15] I can recognize the consistency of his theology with traditional Jewish faith, but it affirms far more in far greater certainty than I can share. Perhaps this contrast makes clear why I believe my position, with all its emphasis on the priority of faith in Judaism, is yet fully a liberal one.

Fourth, from this dynamic process of confronting the claims of the tradition in its fullness, and working out concurrence and dissent, the individual comes to know himself fully. It is not just that Judaism will teach him what a man is and ought to be. In thinking through his disagreements with the tradition, in seeking to justify and explain his necessary difference of opinion, he will find himself revealed. Both Judaism as accepted guide and as rejected standard will call forth the mixture of person and tradition that should mark the modern Jew.

This living interchange between the self and the tradition can thus provide the base from which the individual can reach out to all that diversity of modern life and culture which the tradition could not know. Again the order is reversed. One does not here begin with psychiatry or democracy and come to find what in Judaism agrees with them. Rather, in confrontation with the tradition one creates a matrix of value with which to reach out to modern culture, willing to learn from it where one can, but sufficiently secure not to hesitate to criticize it. The firmer one's roots are in Judaism the freer he will feel to participate in modern society in its most varied activities. Knowing with reasonable clarity who he is and for what he stands, this new Jew can go his way as critic or enthusiast with quiet confidence.

This approach seems to me to be theoretically sound, if by that one means consistent with the faith from which it sprang. It is far more difficult to say whether it can work practically.

The approach sketched out here would need to be discussed in terms of its relation to the Jewish sources, to clarify how it is possible to assert, despite the obvious difficulties, that there is such a thing as an integrated tradition of Jewish belief. True to my faith, I mean that in a Jewish, not a philosophic, way. The polarity of positions may sometimes not make coherent philosophical sense but yet serve the unity perceived by faith. It would also be of value, particularly in view of the vigorous insistence on the priority of faith given here, for me to discuss the significant role reason still retains in this conception of Jewish theology. That would center around the admission of the impossibility of coming to the tradition completely without preconceptions or in explaining it without a frame of meaning. In both cases the aim would be to use reason as fully as possible subject only to prior faith in Judaism. That would lead on to the important role of contemporary philosophy in the work of theology and the way in which various systems might be usefully employed.

But this chapter was devoted to making clear the way in which method necessarily depends upon faith. The critical question is: What is your primary faith? For me that faith is Judaism, and, as a result, I feel that a new methodology is needed in liberal Jewish theology. Men of other basic commitments will take other directions. That is their privilege and their right. If anything can characterize the proposal given here, it is this: For me and for many modern Jews the crucial question of existence has shifted from How can a Jew truly be a modern man? to How can a modern man be truly a Jew?

NOTES: *Chapter 8*

1. Mordecai Kaplan, *The Meaning of God in Modern Jewish Religion* (Jewish Reconstructionist Foundation, 1947), p. 28.
2. Mordecai Kaplan, *The Jewish Reconstructionist Papers* (Behrman's Jewish Book House, 1936), p. 98.

3. Kaplan, *The Meaning of God in Modern Jewish Religion*, p. 84.

4. Levi Olan, *Yearbook* of the Central Conference of American Rabbis for 1962 (1963), p. 238.

5. Levi Olan, *Judaism*, 5.2, Spring, 1956, p. 114.

6. Roland Gittelsohn, *Man's Best Hope* (Random House, Inc., 1961), pp. 61–62.

7. Leo Baeck, *The Essence of Judaism* (The Macmillan Company, 1936), pp. 118–119.

8. Obviously this does not mean that all the content of Judaism is derived from or reached by faith but that its major premises, such as the existence of God, his goodness, the ultimate triumph of righteousness, revelation, election, all involve faith.

9. Gittelsohn, *op. cit.*, p. 62.

10. Mordecai Kaplan, *Judaism as a Civilization* (Jewish Reconstructionist Press, 1957), pp. 36–45.

11. *Ibid.*, pp. 309–310.

12. Olan, *Judaism*, p. 114.

13. Levi Olan, in *Reform Judaism*, essays by alumni of the Hebrew Union College (Hebrew Union College Press, 1949), pp. 28 ff.

14. Olan, *Yearbook*, pp. 226 ff.

15. Although I cannot associate myself with Ben-Horin's own exaggeration and the dogmatism which he brings to his pragmatic criteria, the reader will find a useful collection of some of Heschel's most disturbing habits in Meir Ben-Horin's "The Ultimate and the Mystery" in the *Jewish Quarterly Review*, Vol. LI, No. 1 (July, 1960).

9

AUTONOMY VERSUS TRADITION

THE REFORM of Judaism to meet the situation of an emancipated Jewry became possible only when, even unconsciously, the autonomy of man could be asserted and given precedence over against the authority of Jewish tradition. Because Moses Mendelssohn could do so only in the realm of theology and not in that of practice he remains "orthodox." When Israel Jacobson believed the individual's duty to follow his mind and conscience was more important than following inherited forms of liturgical observances, then the reform could begin. But because Jacobson and other innovators consciously directed their autonomous will to the continuation of historic Judaism, they considered their modification of it itself Judaism. Indeed, if change was once central to Judaism, liberalism is now the most authentic form of Judaism.

Theoretically, the autonomy is prior to the tradition and has hierarchical superiority in matters of decision. Practically, the German liberals were men who used it to renew their Judaism. So they are Liberal, Progressive, or Reform Jews, with the autonomous adjectives modifying the tradition, which remains the continuing substantive term. When Moses Mendelssohn's children and grandchildren could not autonomously affirm Judaism, they followed their enlightened will into the church. Today they would become some variety of secular man. Only now they are so often joined by other refugees from Judaism that they form a Jewish class and it is difficult therefore to tell on which side of the margin of continuing Jewishness they still stand.

This paradox of a logically prior autonomy used to affirm the value of Jewish tradition has, in fact, been basic to all non-orthodox Jewish theology since the early nineteenth century and the source of its inevitable intellectual tensions. Already in Zechariah Frankel and Samuel Holdheim of that time, progressive Judaism had to face the demand for a reactionary or a revolutionary turn. Voices at either extreme are again heard today. By their very opposition to one another they drive the divergent positions yet farther apart and tend to polarize all liberal Jewish thinking. It should be helpful therefore as well as intellectually interesting to explore the problematic of affirming in the present situation the simultaneous value of the autonomous will and Judaism's demands on the Jew.

Liberal Jews should not underestimate their great stake in the concept of autonomy, for it is the source of their special contribution to Judaism. They came into being because they were not content simply to accept what the Jewish past brought to a radically transformed Jewish present. Rather, their forefathers of the nineteenth century had the courage to insist against what their Jewish teachers had taught them, that Judaism's creative adaptiveness through the ages is one of its chief characteristics, and against what the authorities of their community insisted, that it can change. When they did so they defended themselves ultimately on the basis of what Kant had already defined as the key principle of enlightenment: the autonomy of man. The early liberals did not apply the concept as individualistically as did the philosophers of their day or this. The German rabbis wrote and thought more of the autonomy of each generation or epoch, thus validating in a rather corporate way their right to differ from their ghetto forebears. Thus they preserved a community aspect to their sense of rightful change and hoped to avoid the anarchy or defection that would be the fruit of radical individualism. In their reform of Judaism they hoped to fuse the best of the tradition with modern man's sense of truth and value. They tried to shape a Judaism that they felt would stand the scrutiny and fulfill the standards of autonomous man. So they selected and adapted as well as transmitted the Jewish heritage. They stressed prayer in the vernacular, sermons that spoke to mind and heart, instruction for girls as well as boys. They wanted understanding to bring commitment, insight to transform faith by continuity into one of willed acceptance.

It was a grand and noble enterprise. Not so long ago, in the multiple forms of modernized Judaism it had engendered, it seemed to have succeeded nicely. A contemporary style of Judaism has come to seem the most natural thing in the world. Not only do most Jews no longer live in the ghetto manner and yet consider themselves to be loyal Jews, but even the traditionally observant have changed the tone and emphasis of their practice in a way that seemed unthinkable in the early, acrimonious debates.

Alas, that happy balance between modernity and tradition is breaking down. On the one side it is because modern man, under the influence of a secular civilization, has become more radical in his demands for autonomy. Everything is valued in terms of the self, its needs, its fulfillment. Yet, on the other side, the rising rate of intermarriage, poor attendance at prayer, and the general apathy of practice seem to force the admission that if Judaism is to continue in any significant way, it must create a deeper piety and express it in richer observance.

Consider the problem as it arises with teen-agers or college youth, those apostles of individuality. They rebel for more freedom, more independence, the right to be only what they choose to be. Their Jewish teachers know they and their parents are not good enough Jews. The young want greater autonomy. The synagogue wants more Judaism and it defensively tends to see in the cry for more freedom not an appropriate affirmation of human responsibility but a threat to everything it holds dear. For insofar as choice is fully free, it may settle on anything as well as Judaism, and there is enough historic as well as contemporary experience to show that the fear is realistic. Moreover, it would be fantasy to assume that some new philosophic or social scientific answer will quickly solve the problem. Religion is as social and psychological a phenomenon as an intellectual one. Hence the response it gives must be as institutional as it is philosophic, if not more so. For anyone who wants continuing commitment to Judaism, how can the pursuit of autonomy and not Jewish discipline be the ultimate good?

That is the reactionary wing of liberal Judaism speaking, and one hears in its words the instinctive adult response to youthful demands for autonomy: Lay down the law and require its observance. Often this keeps the children in line—for a while. Is that then what progressive Judaism should do? Stem the rising tide of indifference and unconcern by defining necessary beliefs and setting forth required standards of practice?

Were this position only negatively motivated it would have little appeal. Its power stems from the reality of the failure to help liberal Jews understand Jewish belief or instruct them in the value of Jewish observance. How can one expect to win their autonomous assent to Judaism in a world that fights religion and considers Jewish faith odd if they are not given sophisticated, thoughtful guidance as to their living Jewish alternatives in thought and practice? Where are the books on belief and observance serious enough to be considered worthy of review by others than colleagues who owe the author attention?

There is, however, a critical distance between guidance and

authority, between education and legislation. Liberal Judaism was created over precisely this issue, and despite the risks it is difficult to see how it could remain true to itself if it took a dogmatic tack. Where is the theory of revelation which today could authorize by God's own will statements of belief or practice? Is there any human authority to which men should surrender their autonomy? Practically, who would listen to this new insistence on discipline? Surely not the youth, the group about whom most of the worrying is done. They know they are or will be as free as they wish in religious matters. They show it in their attitudes today, in their indifference to campus religious activities of every sort tomorrow. The appeal to tradition for its own sake, the insistence upon authority lest the whole thing fall apart, will only strike them as a typical old man's effort to deprive them of their rights so the aged may stay in power. And their parents are far too much part of the secular world to be any more willing to accept authority. The emancipation of the Jews was based on the secular notion of personal freedom of religion. Having joyously accepted its benefits, Judaism cannot now avoid its risks though they grow increasingly great.

So the call comes from the radical pole to admit that Jews are fully part of the modern world and follow wherever that leads. The appeal here is to the unimpeded pursuit of truth, even should it lead far away from the past. One might argue, somewhat homiletically, that this was always the fundamental concern of Judaism. Was not Abraham the first Jew by virtue of smashing his father's idols and thereby boldly breaking from his religion? This is an age of scientific advance, of intellectual acceleration, of technological conquest. How can Jews remain content to speak in terms of old Semitic or rabbinic mythologies?

The arguments are so familiar they run the risk of being rejected because they have become boring. Yet at this extreme too there is much truth. Surely Judaism has known since the days of the prophets that Jewish survival depends not on old institutions meticulously preserved but on the God of truth served, if need be, by the destruction of his own house. The old intellectual structures of nineteenth-century German idealism which still serve as the staples of modern Jewish liberalism are hardly fit for a world where the great works of Freud and of Einstein are half a century old and Auschwitz and Hiroshima are nearly a quarter of a century gone. There surely needs to be a statement of Jewish faith as adequate to this age as the Neo-Kantian was to pre World War I German liberal Jewry. The problem, of course, is where to find a proper conceptual matrix for such an explication of Judaism.

The older liberalism could believe that the modern secular mind knows a truth worthy of such trust that it should be allowed to determine what is permissible in modern Jewish belief. To reassert such a relatively uncritical dependency on contemporary philosophy or culture after the lessons of the past century and a half of parasitic liberalism seems unfathomably optimistic amidst a secularity whose chief characteristic is realism pressed almost to the point of pessimism. Yet that is what the radicals propose. They keep hoping they can do for this age what the German reformers did a century ago. They reached out into the culture, into general philosophy, and found a means of explaining Judaism in terms of universal truth. That kept Judaism alive then, and only a similar effort can do so today. (How odd to hear such a decidedly Hegelian assertion in the mouths of supposedly post-Hegelians.)

There are two reasons why this will not work again, one intellectual and one social.

When the German reformers sought survival by fusing their Judaism with the *Zeitgeist*, the spirit of the age, they were in an intellectual climate suffused by a Kantian emphasis on the ethical and a Hegelian concern with history. Both were religiously oriented and thus there was available to the early Jewish liberals a secular, rational spirit relatively accommodating to their Judaism. That is what the radicals would like to find today. But how accommodating are the major philosophic structures of today? None of them—naturalism, existentialism, phenomenology, linguistic analysis—offers hospitality to anything like traditional ethics, much less religion or God. Judaism even in its progressive form would have to change itself radically to adjust to any one of them. The German reformers sounded modern to their contemporaries because everyone except the materialists was some kind of idealist then. There was a *Zeitgeist* and they could use it. Today the sacrifices of such reinterpretation would produce little return. There is no detectable, pervasive, single *Zeitgeist*. None of the philosophic styles is or shows signs of becoming dominant. Worse, they partially contradict one another. To select one as the new Jewish language means alienating the adherents of the other positions. One cannot hope to convince most modern men in an age of such philosophic pluralism. One can only choose which minority of intellectuals one wishes to address.

That being so, it will not do to see the purpose of progressive Jewish theology as essentially the elucidation of a proper modern concept of God. That might be the goal set by a Neo-Kantian theology in which ideas are all important and the idea of God plays a central role. In a contemporary world of contrary conceptual systems it is fantasy to hope to create one idea so compelling it will unify most Jews in Jewish belief. It is even more incredible, after the German experience, to believe that knowing such an idea will bring people to live by it, much less bring them to Jewish observance or the love of the people of Israel. The hope that adopting one philosophic style or another will save Judaism is so reductive of the complexities of the situation that it must be considered some sort of rationalist wishful thinking, a delightful contradiction in terms indeed.

These methodological considerations might be extended by asking by what criteria one selects the philosophy that will become the judge of what remains true in Jewish faith. Having dealt with that topic in the previous chapter, I will pass on to the social realities that stand against the radical position.

Modern men, men in every age, do not live by philosophy or hold back on life's major decisions until they have achieved full intellectual clarity concerning them. Most want a rational component in their life-style and moderns seek to amplify it. Our time is often termed postmodern because we have come to realize how little intellect can rule persons, how much we are the creatures of our will and our times. On the surface the German Jewish effort to move with the *Zeitgeist* seemed a straightforward intellectual decision in the Hegelian spirit. Yet it had a most significant social foundation. The early reformers must have sensed that in large part they could depend on their society to encourage ethical religion while setting limits for Jewish assimilation. Accommodation to the culture in their world implied a morally oriented concern with spirit, while negatively its anti-Semitism would keep most Jews within their ancestral community. Besides, their Jews came from an observant community and were surrounded by the historic evidences of their folk past. Many were learned. All had Jewish memories. Their community being deeply Jewish, the thinkers could concentrate on the lessons of autonomy. Their primary thrust is rightly called a Jewish universalism.

That is far from the contemporary Jewish situation. As the secularity of the American society grows, it fortunately has less and less place for overt anti-Semitism and more and more appreciation for Jewish productiveness and creativity. Yet it also has little place for real religion or substantial ethnicity. The rise of democracy and technology means greater freedom for Jews as individuals but less use for them or anyone as a religious community. Indeed, what Judaism must recognize is that contemporary culture is moving toward an amoral, pleasure-seeking, present-oriented human style. One cannot count on educated people to be religious, or spiritual, or even moral when a real crisis occurs. Modern secular society has no institution, no philosophy or even cultural thrust with which to divert or control its inherent drive toward use and payoff. That, not philosophic inadequacy, is the real challenge confronting Judaism. Moreover, one can no longer count on anti-Semitism or sentiment to keep Jews Jewish. Increasingly, American Jews have few rich memories of Jewishness to fall back on as a last, lowest level of Jewish identity. So it is folly for contemporary Jewish thinkers to elaborate a new Jewish universalism in the unconscious hope that social forces may be counted on to keep men ethical, religious, or Jewish, and thereby counteract their centrifugal thrust. Today such a major outward thrust implies what one could hope it did not in nineteenth-century Germany, committing most of the Jewish community to the new American paganism.

For most liberal Jews, I believe, that is too radical a stance. On the minimal level that is because they believe in the lasting significance of what may for the moment be too simply described as ethics. They may consider freedom a great value, but if it leads to moral nihilism, it has vitiated its own virtue. Freedom is not an end in itself, no matter where it leads, as Sartre and other atheist existentialists argue. For most Jews—even those of little faith—autonomy is precious as the precondition of a mature morality. It is itself an ethical commandment; hence, when it is used to destroy ethics, it negates itself.

To hold such a high view of ethical standards in contemporary society is already to share a minority faith. It is no longer widespread in the contemporary civilization and surely not self-evident or rationally demonstrable. Where one is to find the foundation for it in the future becomes increasingly problematic. So when the children of a community that made law precious and the doing of commandment supreme speak against the crowd for freedom confirmed in ethical responsibility, that may properly be understood as the old Jewish faith expressing itself in modern though truncated form.

Others are more positively Jewish. Having given themselves wholeheartedly to contemporary civilization, particularly its high culture and its politics, and having done so to the point of forgetting or forsaking their Judaism, they find themselves betrayed. With all its greatness, with all its promise, there is a stinking rot near the core of Western, industrial, democratic society. The moral revulsion that Jews felt at the Hitlerian destruction of European Jewry could by the nasty be ascribed to Jewish ghetto sensitivity on the one side and German totalitarian madness on the other. Yet the appalling record of the succeeding decades has made it seem more prophetic than exceptional. Wherever one turns—black men, yellow men; the aged, the poor; the military, the industrialists; the educated, the respected—there is violence and exploitation, madness pretending to respectability, infirmity masquerading as competence.

If that is what a good part of today's world is like, then many men will healthfully want to dissociate from it. The Jewish activism remains too strong for adults to drop out with the flower children or by way of drugs. But to identify completely is likely to mean surrendering values that now suddenly are as dear as they are nonconforming. The cultivation of a proper alienation has become a human necessity. So Jewish roots become a needed source of strength and Jewish forms of expression a helpful way of reaffirming self by taking one's distance from the majority. Having a Jewishness to assert against a freedom gone wild has suddenly become a precious privilege as even the novelists have now discovered.

These realities reestablish the classic paradox of liberal Jewish theology. Only now, so to speak, there must be a change in its social orientation. Jewish universalism has had its day. It has shown, and indispensably so, that Jews can be modern. Now it is time to move to the next task. What is required is a stress on Judaism strong enough to serve as an antidote for paganism and an appreciation of man powerful enough to make him recognize how much of his fulfillment depends upon himself. That sense of partnership between man and God was basic to the traditional Jewish belief in the Covenant. Yet it strikes a progressive, liberal note in giving man a greater share in its working out—and if God's absence in the Hitler days taught Judaism nothing, it should have taught Jews they must do just that. What is needed today in liberal Judaism, then, is what I propose to call an open traditionalism.

It cannot be a simple reiteration of classic Jewish faith, for what has been learned from a century and a half of progressive Judaism cannot be denied. Traditional Jews had once become so dependent upon God and his saving power that they seemed to have forgotten how to help themselves. They were abjectly passive before social injustice and historical abuse. They could only go to Palestine to die, not to rebuild themselves or the Jewish people. The Reform movement came into being in reaction to that denigration of man. Its history has legitimated, in a way that cannot be gainsaid, the modern Jew's fundamental concern for autonomy. So this reasserted traditionalism must be open, recognizing the basic importance of the free choice of human action, including, therefore, the right to conscientious dissent from what Jewish tradition once required or strongly urged.

Such openness led the early reformers to place all their trust in man and his creativity. They were self-confident and optimistic about society. It was enough for God to be an integrating moral idea. History was man's province. In the light of later events their faith seems childish and naïve, an overcompensation against traditional belief as understandable for them as it is unacceptable today. Jewish humanism with religious trimmings and certainly more radical forms of openness will not do at this moment of crisis in civilization. So the openness affirmed here is first directed inward toward Jewish belief and practice. Historic Judaism is claimed as the ground of one's personal existence, yet in that act the right to dissent is carried along. If the differences with the tradition which arise become fundamental, they might shatter the essential paradoxicality of the stand and a radical individualism would have to be reasserted. Or one might discover there was a principle of dissent which represented the highest truth to which one's autonomy was pledged. Liberals would have great respect for either of those outcomes though they might lead the searching soul out of Judaism. For the reasons given above, it can be hoped that this will not become the common case for those reestablishing their Jewish faith. It should also be noted that there is another possibility which might occur. It might turn out that the individual discovers he has no reason to dissent from the tradition whatsoever and is, in fact, orthodox. Liberals should see in such an autonomously reclaimed orthodoxy a surprising but a happy Jewish result indeed.

This emphasis on tradition, though open, makes it possible to believe that for the first time in liberal Jewish history a reverse relation to the culture may become possible, that Jewish faith may now be legitimated as its possible critic. Ever since the emancipation, the judgment has come steadily from the outside. It was enough to make one wonder whether there was anything in Jewish faith that could stand up against a widely held modern belief. Now Judaism becomes precious for just that which once made it undesirable, its quality of alienation and transcendence of the society.

This has direct application to the problem of relating Judaism and philosophy. In this new approach to Jewish thought it is the tradition, openly held, which is the most important criterion of the philosophy used to interpret it. Which of the modern options is most congenial to its content, not which is most widely held or persuasively represented on campus this decade, determines the mode of doing theology in an open traditionalism. In terms of my Jewish affirmations, religious existentialism is the most complementary philosophic style available. It supplies the hermeneutic instrument for interpreting Judaism in modern terms but may not usurp that role as a means to replace the primacy of traditional Jewish faith for me. That is what this self-conscious commitment to open traditionalism clarifies. Now when the religious existentialist insights contradict what study shows is classic Jewish faith, as is true in the areas of society, history, and law, I do not automatically judge Judaism to be wrong. Rather, I investigate to see what it is that I truly affirm. Perhaps I believe as the existentialists do and thereby discover a principle to my dissent and thus a higher faith which I affirm. Perhaps here I do autonomously uphold traditional belief and am thus led to criticize and correct religious existentialism. In the case of society and history it seems to me the existentialists are wrong and need the interpersonal, time-oriented vision which Jewish faith provides. In the case of law I dissent from both positions. That leads me to a Jewish sense that all authentic existence must be structured, an understanding foreign to existentialism. Yet I am also moved to an existentialist reworking of Jewish law in personalist terms it could not traditionally tolerate.

It is also important to keep in mind that this approach is not normally static. Openness implies new ideas, new insight, new consideration, the ongoing process of again and again winning one's traditionalism by personal affirmation. There is no guarantee that what is cherished today will not be discarded tomorrow. That is the risk of freedom without which mature humanity is unobtainable.

An open traditionalism would necessarily shake itself into incompatible pieces if it tried to come into being primarily as either a body of coherent doctrine, as the radicals generally prescribe, or as a body of required practice, as the reactionaries insist. The former is too abstract to tolerate paradox; the latter, too specific to tolerate freedom. What is needed rather is something far more existential, what may be termed style. Without sophistication one has behavior but not style. Without structure one is only erratic. In recognizable style, mind and action interpenetrate, integrating in life what if left to mind alone would be paradox. The present stage of Jewish theology should work toward the creation and definition of this modern style of Jewish being. One way of doing so is to show through analysis that the fundamental dialectic of such a style is not a matter of arbitrary decision but a necessary relatedness in the two basic faiths.

The key to such a demonstration comes from the recognition that any life lived in devotion to autonomy must, despite a cool exterior or a therapeutic humor, at some point reach a sense of high seriousness. Playing superautonomy demands dedication to survive. A casual concern with it in this culture means its speedy demise, a self-contradiction not to be resolved. Modern Judaism, however, can be hospitable to the autonomous approach because it knows that when man faces himself in ultimate seriousness he stands ready to transcend himself. Man cannot serve as the ground of his own dignity. He is not self-explanatory or self-justifying. The question Who is man? leads on, if it is radically affirmative, to Who is God? Anthropology in depth is the contemporary way to theology.

Seriousness means that at some point in seeking to be true to oneself one turns back upon one's assumptions with enough power to ask radical questions about them. What is the faith implicit in the passion for autonomy? What commitments ground the right of the person to take himself and to be taken by others with such seriousness? Those become the critical questions on the way to reconciling the paradox.

The individual may claim that his concern for his autonomy was simply his own idea, that it is a self-validating, willed value. Yet if it is important to make a similar assertion for all men, if such a universal sense of autonomy should be one of the most fundamental considerations in organizing society, then it will not do to rest such comprehensive weight on so arbitrary a basis. For one may well ask in all seriousness today as one would have hesitated to do in more liberalistic times, Why should anyone affirm himself? Most people know themselves to be in many respects deeply unworthy of high regard. That is not a neurotic symptom. After all one's childish fantasies have been brought to consciousness and made to face reality, one may still wonder at one's worth. Even the mature continually fail to meet their own standards or the reasonable demands of those they love. Self-acceptance is one of the great moral and psychic commandments of this era—precisely because it is so difficult if men are expected to be realistic about themselves and what they ought to be.

The imperative to be autonomous cannot be grounded in oneself and surely not in a culture that regularly tramples on it. Nor does the faith of every religion lead to it. Confucius would have men bend the self to the old social values. Lao-tzu asks that the self empty itself so the way of nature may become its way. Hinduism would lose the soul in the World Soul. Buddhism does not consider the self a reality to be enhanced and strengthened. Only in Judaism and its daughter religions does autonomy become possible, indeed necessary.

The Hebrews know man as the single creature who is formed in God's image and bound to God as Covenant partner. Not even his sins break that relationship as his punishment by God under the Covenant shows. That is how radically the worth of his existence is asserted. Yet the Covenant relationship does not require man to surrender himself or to escape from self. Rather, he must affirm his selfhood to participate in it, for it is made with him quite specifically as man. He is not asked to be an angel to fulfill his part in it. Its commandments call him to be only what a man can be. In the rabbinic understanding, man is not only the focus of the commandments but the master of their elaboration against all miracles or other supposed divine intervention. Under such a covenant, man can in rare instances stand on his rights as partner and question even God. His more normal role is to accept God's sovereignty and live by God's law. That he always remains free to accept or reject. Even against God, man has a certain autonomy.

That traditional understanding is not the same as modern man's sense of autonomy, since there the superior status of the Divine and the specificity of his revealed will tend to keep man's freedom to respond at a minimum. Still it is the root whence, by way of Greek abstraction and modern rationalist universalization, it grew to the affirmation of each man's moral dignity. Jewish faith still knows such a God and such a relationship of acceptance and obligation with man. That is the theological root of its contemporary moral disgust. Moreover, Judaism has had extraordinary experience in translating this faith into a daily way of life. It has had such success that Jewish patterns still substantially survive in the general human concerns of Jewish lives despite widespread disbelief and nonobservance. So the Jewish child receives that special welcome and concern which befits a new manifestation of the divine image. Each Jew is pressured to study or to earn because great value is attached to his working out his unique capacities. The family and the community form the social matrix which keeps this attitude toward persons alive and functioning. Intense folk bonds keep the people an identifiable community linked to its ancient traditions though history has been cruel and perfidious. With all its fostering of commonalities, this is a people of fierce individualists, a folk who glory in argument and abhor hierarchy. If autonomy is precious in an antipersonal society, then being Jewish gives one the kind of faith, the sort of life, the community support, the historic experience which makes it possible even today. It is not clear where else in the modern world, except in Christianity, one might otherwise find adequate substantiation for man's vigorous affirmation of his autonomy.

So the paradox of living by autonomy and tradition simultaneously may now be resolved. That does not take the form of subordinating one of the affirmations to the other as both the radicals and reactionaries desire but rather by showing that neither can claim priority over the other. Each depends on its polar opposite. Jewish faith increasingly cannot be the passive continuation of a social heritage which is what it essentially was in previous Jewish generations. The more modern one is, the more one insists that it is a matter of responsible willing. One should choose to be Jewish and resist as nondeterminative the claims of family, history, or personal sentiment. That choice, particularly since it is a fundamental commitment of one's life, must be made autonomously to be authentic. Yet the high value attached to autonomy is no longer self-explanatory. One can explain one's seriousness about it and one's determined pursuit of it only in terms of a prior faith: for the Jew, Judaism. The tradition grounds the autonomy—but it must be the basis of affirming the tradition—and so endlessly. The circle of faith is complete and in its harmonious closing the integrity of liberal Jewish existence despite its paradoxical foundation is established.

EPILOGUE

10

IS IT POSSIBLE TO WRITE A JEWISH THEOLOGY TODAY?

When Kaufmann Kohler in the period before World War I began to write what was to be the first self-conscious, modern theology of Judaism it did not occur to him to ask whether it was possible to do such a thing. Though he called the early, German edition of his book a *Grundriss,* a basic outline, he unconditionally entitled the later English version *Jewish Theology.* His claim to be describing Jewish faith comprehensively is brought out in the title's afterphrase, "Systematically and Historically Considered." Not only did he propose to present Jewish belief in terms of its present content but in its historic development as well. Kohler could assume such a task not only because of his extraordinary grasp of every aspect of contemporary Jewish scholarship but because he knew (in a way that seemed so obvious it hardly required stating much less demonstrating) that historic progress refined truth. Since he stood so knowledgeably at the end of that evolution, he could know what was permanently true in Judaism and how it had been expressed through the ages.

Surely one reason why Kohler receives so little consideration in Jewish theological discussions today is that neither such historical nor theological certainty is any longer available. Half a century of research and contemplation has complicated and confused historic judgments that once seemed simple and clear. Even critical facts are not so unambiguous as they once appeared to be. If data is insisted upon rather than informed surmise, if progressive development is not a reliable rule for reconstructing what really took place, if plural causation and the unexpected are the most useful principles of historic interpretation, it is surprising how little is known for sure about the growth of Jewish belief.

Already there, the contemporary philosophic problems assert themselves. History is no longer simple because the criteria by which it should be structured are uncertain and debated. Even when there are patterns of interpretation in use it is not clear whether these are adopted by analogy to game theory as the arbitrary rules by which one pursues a given academic activity, or as a reflection of reality and therefore represent a claim for metaphysical truth ordering time and finitude. For just as history no longer shows a single progressive march of Jewish faith, so contemporary philosophy does not provide a single standard of truth so widely accepted that it might become the foundation of a theology of Judaism. Amidst this cultural confusion the faith and practice of American Jews are themselves so loose and changing that they cannot provide an unambiguous basis for Jewish theology. With history unclear, philosophy uncertain, and Judaism in men's lives unsure of itself, Kohler's project is today unthinkable.

It is not easily evident that even *a* Jewish theology could be articulated under present conditions. The shift to *a* implies the recognition that a measure of subjectivity is involved, that no claim is made to speak for the Jewish tradition without mediation of self. That mitigates the problem somewhat. Nonetheless, that article implies unity, and that integrity as well as comprehensiveness is present in the discussion of Judaism. Whence can that structure derive? Where does the individual interpreter now find the framework he proposes to use for expounding Judaism and the method by which he will explicate its old truths in a modern yet authentic way? None of the old answers will do, and no new ones that will decisively correct these failings seem in the offing.

Perhaps, then, one should only do theology rather than try to write a theology. That would mean working on individual themes without being concerned too much about what interconnects them. Not every generation has it in its power to synthesize, and this may be a time in which partial concerns thoughtfully pursued will be more fruitful than a premature effort to relate them one to the other. Approaching Jewish theology by way of significant fragments today may in the more settled situation of another generation make possible a statement of the integrity of Judaism as a whole that is now impractical.

Prudence would dictate that approach, but there are intellectual and moral reasons that might make even a failure at the comprehensive effort more desirable. Form has a vital role to play in theology, and its effect on content is considerable. One's attitude toward Jewish ethnicity is decisively altered if one makes the Jewish people the bearer of a universally available idea of God as in Baeck, or the source of a socially necessary idea as in Kaplan, or the Covenant partner of God as in Buber. Jewish law is God-given to Heschel, folk-created in different ways to Baeck and Kaplan, and man-created out of dialogue with God to Buber. Its authority and continuing content vary from case to case. Not to see the total perspective of faith in which a given aspect of Jewish faith is held is therefore not really to understand the implications of that belief. One must try to see the whole to appreciate the fragments.

Besides, there is a sense in which the integrity of Jewish belief is a moral imperative. That occurs in the life of the believing Jew. If he is a man whose personal existence is founded on his Jewish belief, one whose actions are in continual touch with his fundamental commitment to Judaism—both realized imperfectly at any one time and only with varying levels of success as the time passes—he knows an integrity to Judaism through his integrity of self. For him to be true to self means likewise to be true to the Judaism from which his self is not divisible. As a man he must think about who he is, but for him that means simultaneously thinking about what his Judaism is. As he seeks a growing unity of self, so he will seek a coherence to his Judaism. Such a man must do Jewish theology if only to be true to himself. He would aspire to do a Jewish theology then as one way of answering the command to be a person, single and whole even as his God is one and not fragmented. Because he is a Jew he does not carry on that task as only an isolated self but as part of the people of Israel, responsive to its tradition, loyal to its God.

That task, though improbable, is not impossible. The unitary stance developed here and applied to a variety of problems in my forthcoming companion volume, *How Can a Jew Speak of Faith Today?* gives reason to hope that with greater extension and depth it might serve as a responsible basis for undertaking the holistic task.

Any effort to confront the classic faith of Jewish tradition will be too superficial and evaluative for the historians. Doing so in the name of self rather than in terms of some abstract statement of truth will be too existential and subjective for the philosophers. Giving primary attention to the claims of the tradition will be too Jewish and restricted for the personalist radicals. There are many people who cannot accept the fundamental premises of such an approach and to whom it therefore cannot speak. They may even be a majority of the thinking community. Yet in so difficult an intellectual and religious time as this such an effort should probably be judged less in terms of the answers it provides than in terms of the response it evokes. If it can stimulate serious, learned discussion and be an existential as well as an intellectual challenge as to what it might mean to do Jewish theology, then it will have been as communally useful as it is personally necessary. The previous generation of Jewish thinkers gave us their answers and the inspiration of their example. The present task, born of their greatness and a movement away from their certainties, may be simply to bequeath a legacy of worthy questions for the rising generation to confront and perhaps to answer.